activities & projects:
MEXICO
in color

By Claude Soleillant

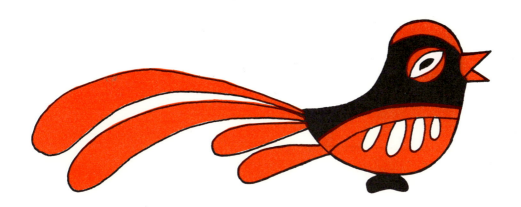

STERLING PUBLISHING CO., INC. NEW YORK

Oak Tree Press Co., Ltd. London & Sydney

BOOKS OF INTEREST

Aluminum & Copper Tooling

Costumes from Crepe Paper

Felt Crafting

Mexico in Pictures

Pin Pictures

Starting with Papier Mâché

You Can Put On a Show

Translated by Steven Morgenstern
Photos by Christian Murtin

The original edition of this book was published in France
under the title, "Activités aux couleurs du . . . Mexique"
© 1976 by Editions Fleurus, Paris.

Second Printing, 1979
Copyright © 1977 by Sterling Publishing Co., Inc.
Two Park Avenue, New York, N.Y. 10016
Distributed in Australia and New Zealand by Oak Tree Press Co., Ltd.,
P.O. Box J34, Brickfield Hill, Sydney 2000, N.S.W.
Distributed in the United Kingdom and elsewhere in the British Commonwealth
by Ward Lock Ltd., 116 Baker Street, London W 1
Manufactured in the United States of America
All rights reserved
Library of Congress Catalog Card No.: 77-81955
Sterling ISBN 0-8069- 4552-4 Trade   Oak Tree 7061- 2560-6
4553-2 Library

CONTENTS

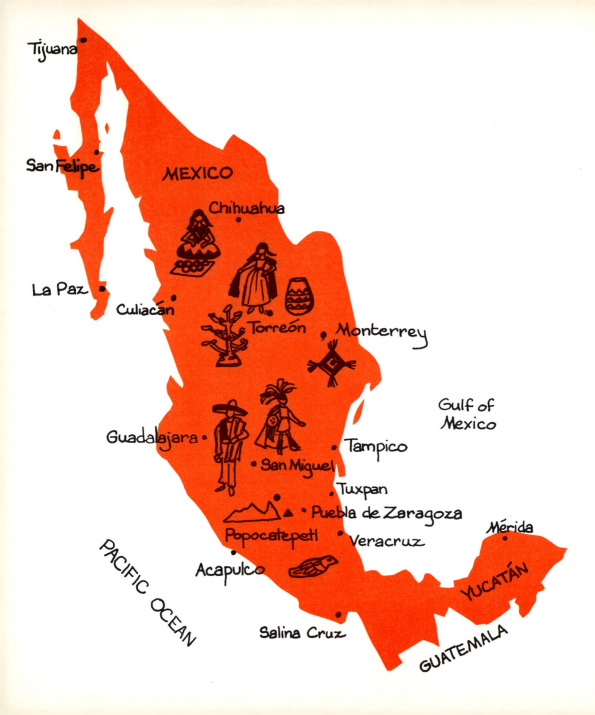

INTRODUCTION

Mexico is a land rich in reminders of the past. It was the home of the ancient pre-Hispanic civilizations, which strongly influenced the nation and the world with their achievements in a wide range of subjects: mathematics, astronomy, architecture, sculpture and, of course, handicrafts.

In a more everyday realm, Mexico introduced corn, cocoa, tomatoes, pimentos and the wild turkey to Europe.

The folklore of Mexico is also extremely rich and varies widely from one area to another because of the differences in history and geographical conditions in the various regions. Don't forget that Mexico is very large, with an area of more than 760,000 square miles (2,000,000 km²).

Needless to say, we are not going to try to present all aspects of Mexican folklore in this book, but rather to give you enough background and information so that, in a few hours, you can get some feeling for the richness of the culture.

To help more, you will find in the back of this book the addresses of Mexican tourist information offices which will be happy to supply interested students with information about their country.

You will find different activities in this book which can be brought together in an exciting Mexican festival or fair. The get-together you plan can be as simple or as complicated as you want to make it: an unusual party for a few people, an outdoor festival, or an entertaining program for a group of children or young people are just a few possibilities.

In this book you will find:

costumes	ideas for decorations
games	a story to read or act out
food	a plan for a Mexican fair
things to make	Mexican dances

All of these should combine to provide a Mexican experience which is artistic, active, festive, attractive and exciting.

A MEXICAN FESTIVAL

This can be a spectacular party including songs, dances, games, story-telling, acting and other activities. In order to give the proceedings structure, we will group these activities on the following pages as parts of a Mexican marketplace scene. It will only be necessary to give you a few suggestions, since you will want to arrange your festival according to the location available, the abilities and desires of the people involved and possibly also the information you have acquired while studying the Mexican nation.

What is important here is to provide a framework and a linking element to the presentation of the activities that will follow. The linking element in the marketplace is the master of ceremonies, who will explain the scene and introduce the action.

His script must be very free and support the "extras" who fill the spaces between activities with entrances and exits and improvised miming of everyday market scenes: shopping, moving about, gossiping, and so on.

These "extras" can participate in the games and possibly in dances, and must pay careful attention to the presentation of stories by other actors.

ATMOSPHERE AND DECORATION

Represent a very gay and colorful marketplace by using very simple elements. You should try to capture the *feeling* of the marketplace, and not aim for an exact reproduction. At the back and sides of the scene stack boxes and cartons to represent market stalls on which are found some of the items for which instructions are given in this book, and possibly other things:

● Multicolored fabrics, scarves, sheets.

● Examples of basketry

● Imaginative jewelry

● Pottery, preferably of red clay. These can be replaced by plastic pots painted with red ochre gouache or, even simpler, with silhouettes of pots and vases cut from cardboard and painted in red ochre.

● Fruits and vegetables, either papier mâché or made with newspaper in rough shapes and covered with crepe paper.

If possible, stretch large white bedsheets over the stalls, suspending them on poles and anchoring them at the bottom corners with strings tied to rocks.

To start off, place woven mats directly on the ground. On the mats put baskets three-quarters full of crumpled newspaper and, on top, visible to the eye, place real fruits and vegetables: oranges, bananas, tomatoes, peppers, onions, and so on.

Complete the scene with some large green potted plants.

Reserve a space in the middle for the dances and games.

If the festival will take place indoors or at night, arrange for a good lighting set-up, with a small spotlight for the dances.

Also arrange for a phonograph and Mexican records to provide background music.

CHARACTERS AND COSTUMES

You can have as many characters as you like, young and old, men and women, boys and girls.

The women should wear simple Mexican costumes:

● Skirts in bright colors gathered at the waist

● Tee-shirts in matching or contrasting colors

● Large scarves in deep blue or black with fringes

Hairstyles: braids in real hair or black wool, parted in the middle.

The men may wear white pants or light-blue jeans and short-sleeved shirts.

If possible, they should each wear a *poncho* or small blanket or rag rug in bright colors folded over their shoulders.

Everyone should wear espadrilles or leather sandals.

To perform the dances, the dancers can simply be dressed as described above or they can wear more elaborate costumes. The girls, for instance, can wear Costume No. 1 described on page 40, and the boys can wear the traditional costume on page 34.

For the "Dance of the Devil" the dancers can dress up as shown in the drawing here:

● White pants tied at the ankle

● If possible, red culottes made from crepe paper or felt over the pants

● White, long-sleeved shirt with red crepe-paper sash

● High, cone-shaped hat made of cardboard. Decorate it with crossed strips and streamers of red, green and blue crepe paper. Hold the hat in place with elastic under the chin, if necessary.

ACTION

If the festival takes place on a stage with a curtain, begin by playing a record of Mexican music as the curtain opens. If the festival is taking place in a room indoors or at night outdoors, darken the lights. Then, in either case, quickly turn on all the lights.

As soon as the lights are on, the "extras" enter in a playful mood and go to the market stalls, some as vendors and some as buyers. The women walk from one stall to another and bargain. The market should become progressively more lively. A merchant can sell ices, crying *"Helados!"* (Spanish for "ices"). There must be lots of noise, lots of chattering, lots of movement. The master of ceremonies (wearing a dark blue shirt, white pants, straw hat with a broad brim) leaves the crowd, walks towards the audience and begins to introduce the action. As soon as he speaks, the "extras" are silent and move about much more slowly, but do not stop completely.

Master of ceremonies: "The market day is a festive day. The shoppers sometimes come from far away to buy supplies. The stalls are

cardboard cone

crepe paper

well stocked and the hanging sheets block out the fiery sun.

"But the most popular parts of the marketplace are the dancers, the musicians, the storytellers . . . the crowd gathers around them to watch and listen.

"The music is beginning now, and the boys are choosing their partners . . . . Everyone in place for the dance!"

Dance, for example, the *"Raspa"* described on page 55.

The dancers leave the crowd of extras, who stand in a large semi-circle.

The boys invite the girls, who remained in the crowd, to dance, and lead them to the middle of the circle. They dance 1 or 2 dances.

They can finish with the "Dance of the Devil," a dance which can be improvised by the boy dancers who have a good sense of rhythm, since all that's involved is a sort of mime game. One of the dancers plays the devil. He wears a mask (see the drawing on page 8) and a red cape. The other dancers can dress as described earlier.

Moving to a lively folk song, the devil attacks the other dancers, who jump, dodge and leap to escape. Then the dancers take sticks (rolls of paper tied with string) passed to them by the bystanders and take their turn attacking the devil. He tries to ward off their blows. Then the dance ends with the pursuit of the devil, who disappears in the market crowd.

The "extras" begin walking around.

Master of ceremonies: "There they are! Our dancers have certainly earned a moment's rest.

"But look . . . who is arriving? It's Juan, the joker, who always has a trick in his bag to amuse the idlers and win a few coins."

A man in multicolored costume enters carrying in his hand a basket covered with a rag and, in the other hand, a long stick with a string, to which is attached a *piñata* (see page 28).

Juan: "Hello! Hello, *amigos.* Who would like to play with the *piñata*? Who wants to win the magnificent prizes I have here in my basket?

"Come now, gentlemen, one small *peso* for the joy of winning the marvels in my basket of secrets. There aren't enough to go around . . . Hurry up! One *peso* . . . one *peso.* . . ."

The "extras" crowd around and mime the gesture of giving money. Then Juan organizes the *Piñata* Game as it is described on page 50, except that he shakes the *piñata* attached to the string like a fisherman who dangles the bait before the fish. A few people can play the game. They should move quickly or the spectators will become bored.

When the game is finished, the players congratulate each other while Juan gathers his equipment and tries to disappear in the crowd.

But the winners stop him and try to claim their prizes. The juggler insists that nobody won . . . they argue.

One of the players grabs the basket and removes the cover . . . the basket is empty!

The players and the crowd all complain. The juggler escapes in the confusion. Little by little the crowd quiets down.

It is also possible, instead of playing the *piñata* game, to choose 1 or 2 of the other games described. It is a good idea to present as much action as possible.

Once again the crowd begins moving around the stage. They stop in place and listen to something. The sound of the Indian flute is heard, softly at first, then louder.

An old man (or an actor impersonating one) enters. He wears strange ragged garments.

He wears a *sarape* and mimes the action of playing the flute.

The crowd scatters and lets him walk to the foreground, where he sits on a stool while the crowd groups around him. Some of the group members can sit on the ground.

Master of ceremonies: "It is not a market day without a storyteller. Here is old Pepe, who always has a legend to tell to the waiting crowd."

Storyteller: "Good people, good people, the road was long and old Pepe is very tired. A small glass of *tequila* would help me to refresh my memory and bring you some story to make you rejoice or make you dream."

They give him a glass of *tequila* (water).

"Friends, many years have passed in our ancient Mexican land, and long ago . . . what happened was . . . I remember . . ."

Here he tells the legend of Popocatepetl (see page 60) or another Mexican story. When the story is over, old Pepe picks up his flute and leaves the stage with short, shuffling steps.

As he exits, the master of ceremonies steps forward to conclude: "This is the scene at the Mexican marketplace. Of course, if your curiosity should someday take you to this ancient and beautiful land, you will not find our old Pepe at a street corner, nor the trickster with his *piñata* game. But what does it matter? You have sampled some of the pleasures of a foreign land here in our own country, and know a little bit more about your world."

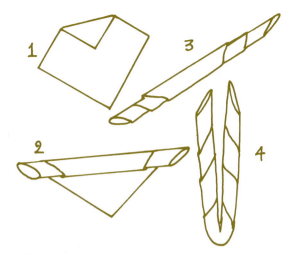

A MEXICAN MEAL

DECORATION

Mexican meals should take place outdoors whenever possible, since the food is often cooked over a wood fire. The barbecue style of cooking, which has become very popular all around the world, began in Mexico. In rural areas the people cook over terra-cotta braziers filled with charcoal.

The pots the food is cooked in are also made of terra-cotta. Certain foods are prepared on an ordinary barbecue grill or over a wood fire in a pit dug in the ground.

Skewers or spits are balanced between bricks, standing high enough above the coals so the food doesn't burn.

For the table, if you are going to serve food at your festival, use a large wooden board placed over a set of carpenters' horses. Cover it with a white paper tablecloth, in a pattern to imitate damask linen if you can find one. Around the table place folding garden chairs, wooden chairs or long wooden benches.

The table decorations must be very colorful. Use stoneware or earthenware plates and pitchers and cups in enamelled terra-cotta

if you can get them. Try to find utensils with a rustic look.

You can add colorful highlights to your decoration by making hand-painted vases (page 29), candleholders (page 30) and bird-shaped place-cards (page 30).

You can also make lacy place mats for each setting by cutting out and notching bright sheets of crepe paper.

The napkins should also be bright and colorful. Roll them and fold them as shown in Drawings 1—4. Place the folded napkins in the cups on the table.

The food should be served, if possible, on terra-cotta platters. It has been said that the *tortilla*, a broad thin cake made from corn-flour, like a pancake, serves the Mexican as his bread, plate, spoon and napkin . . . but it's more practical to have a knife and fork at each place setting.

If the meal is being served indoors, hide the furniture (if there is any) under bedsheets decorated with circles of colored paper notched and cut out to look like lace.

chile (sauce made with powdered red chili peppers).

Tortillas are crisp flat cakes made with cornflour which serve as the basis for all of the Mexican meals. Mexicans usually deep-fry them in hot oil, but it is easier (and safer) to cook them on a griddle, like pancakes.

You can serve *tortillas* with all sorts of foods: meats, shrimp, black olives and so forth, or garnished with sauces (like *guacamole*, which can be found on page 91).

Spanish Hot Chocolate is made of powdered cocoa dissolved in hot milk with cinnamon and sugar added.

The Mexicans use many tomatoes and avocados in their dishes, as well as fresh fish, sometimes marinated but uncooked as in *ceviche.*

You can add an exotic atmosphere with potted green plants and wicker baskets filled with fruits like pineapples and mangoes.

At each side of the entrance, hang long strings of garlic bulbs or onions, tied together with raffia.

In addition, you can make attractive orange boughs for the doorway by covering plastic foam balls with orange crepe paper. String these balls together along with some green leaves to decorate the entire doorframe (see the drawing).

FOOD

Mexican food includes a wide variety of dishes. You will find recipes for many of the traditional dishes in the Appendix on page 90.

There are many spicy sauces seasoned with

SMALL FESTIVAL

If your Mexican festival is smaller and will take place indoors, plan to use boxes as seats.

Cover them with blankets (or wide sheets of crepe paper) decorated with Mexican designs.

Arrange wicker baskets and terra-cotta pottery (flowerpots, for example) around the room. You can also paint various pottery shapes on cardboard, cut them out and place them against the wall. Hang colorful travel posters on the wall. You can get these by writing to the Mexican Tourist Office (page 94), or from a local travel agent.

Complete the wall decorations with painted panels like those shown on the following pages and with a few of the projects described in the chapter "Things to Make" (page 65).

Mexican artists paint extremely beautiful designs on thin sheets of cork (a replica of one of these paintings is shown in the background of the photo on page 24). The designs are simple but very decorative. They can be imitated simply by painting with gouache on cork panels. These small panels, if they are skilfully done, can be sold if your festival includes a "sale" event.

Other attractive examples of Mexican artwork are found in the masks made from thin metal. These may inspire you to make your own embossed masks from thin metal sheets glued to cardboard backings.

Try to borrow large potted plants, ferns, or artificial plants (you can make your own from crepe paper). A few large cacti cut out of cardboard will add a nice Mexican atmosphere.

EMBOSSED METAL MASK AND PANEL

On this page and on pages 20 and 84 you will find suggestions for Mexican designs which you can make into decorative masks and panels.

Materials

● A thick magazine

● Cardboard sheets

● Sheets of lightweight metal (aluminum or copper for tooling, which you can purchase in a hobby shop)

● A dried-out ballpoint pen; well-rounded paintbrush handle; scissors with sharp points; black china marker; pencil

● Glue

● Sheet of cotton fabric

Construction

● Place a sheet of thin metal on a

magazine. Draw the design you've chosen lightly with a black china marker, without pressing down, and go over the outline with a pencil.

● With the point of a ballpoint pen trace

the important parts of the silhouette, pressing down lightly (you don't want to push through the metal sheet). Make the strongest lines with the handle of a paint-brush.

As you work, remember that each indented line you make appears as a raised line on the other side, which is the side you will display. From time to time it is a good idea to turn the work over and judge the effect of your efforts. A few lines pressed into the front side will make the relief lines stand out.

● Then, if you are making a mask, cut the embossed shape out of the full sheet. Use scissors to carefully cut out the holes for the eyes and mouth. An example of a completed mask and an interesting way to use it is on page 84.

● Instead of cutting out the embossed shape you can keep the square or rectangular shape of the metal and, to protect the thin sheet, glue it onto a piece of cardboard slightly smaller than the metal.

● Before glueing, put a thin layer of cotton fabric between the metal and the cardboard to heighten the relief effect.

● Cut the corners of the metal at an angle and fold the excess over the edge of the cardboard.

SPOTTED PIGEON

You can use this attractive pigeon as a table decoration, or make several and hang them in a mobile.

Materials
● Cardboard sheets

● 2 rectangles of tissue paper, one 10½ x 24¾ inches (26 x 62 cm), the other 14¼ x 13 inches (36 x 33 cm)

● Red and blue felt pieces at least as big as the size of this page, one piece each color

● Fabric glue and white glue

● Nylon fishing line

● Tracing paper

● Soft black pencil or marking pen

Construction

BODY
● Trace the pattern shown on this page onto a sheet of tracing paper. Transfer the shape onto a piece of cardboard. Cut it out neatly.

● Place the cardboard cutout on a piece of blue felt. Trace the outside edges of the pattern with a soft black pencil or marking pen.

● Place the cardboard on the red felt and follow the same procedure.

● Cut out the two felt silhouettes.

WINGS

● Take the 10½ x 24¾ inch (26 x 62 cm) rectangle of tissue paper and fold into accordion pleats, with equal folds ¾ inch (2 cm) wide (see Drawing 1).

● When the sheet is completely folded, fold the band you have made in half and cut across the middle (Drawing 2).

The wings are ready to be glued in place.

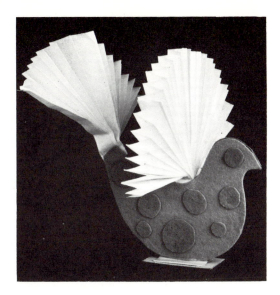

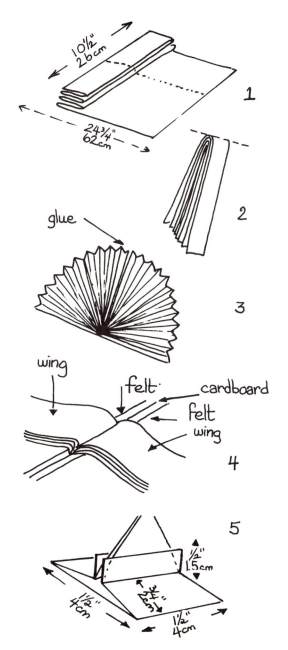

TAIL

● Take the $14\frac{1}{4}$ x 13 inch (36 x 33 cm) piece of tissue paper and make accordion pleats in the same way.

● Fold the pleated band in half and glue the opposite sides together to form a fan shape (Drawing 3).

ASSEMBLY

● Spread glue on the two sides of the cardboard silhouette and glue the felt cutouts in place.

● Slip the ends of the wings between the felt and the cardboard (Drawing 4).

● Glue the tail in place between the felt and the cardboard in the back.

● Pierce a hole near the wings and thread the fishing line through. Make several tight knots.

● Glue felt circles of different sizes on the

body of the bird, using the opposite color on each side: red circles on the blue body and blue circles on the red.

If you want to stand the bird up instead of hanging it, make a cardboard base. Take a cardboard rectangle $4\frac{1}{2}$ x $1\frac{1}{2}$ inches (11 x 4 cm) and fold it as shown in Drawing 5. Cut the angles shown by the dotted lines and glue the tabs in place under the felt on each side of the cardboard.

DECORATIVE GARLANDS

(The hanging garland is shown in color on page 13.)

This garland can be used in many different ways, in long and short lengths.

You can hang several garlands of different lengths from the ceiling, or string extra-long garlands from one side of the room to the other to make a kind of curtain or partition.

Several small garlands can be linked together to make mobiles, as simple or complicated as you like.

Materials

● Copper wire

● Florist's wire (for artificial flowers) or coat-hanger wire

● Nylon fishing line

● Wooden beads of different sizes, at least $\frac{1}{2}$–$\frac{3}{4}$ inch (1–2 cm) in diameter.

● Strips of thin cardboard or oaktag, $\frac{3}{4}$–$1\frac{1}{4}$ inch (2–3 cm) wide and 10–14 inches (25–35 cm) long. Bend them into rings, staple the ends together and paint with gouache or poster paints.

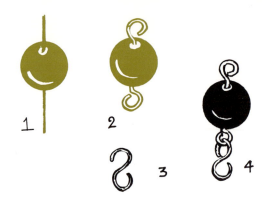

● Cutting pliers, round-nose pliers

● Stapler

Construction

The garlands are made up of several different pieces, assembled one within another. The pieces you use will vary according to your taste and the materials available. You can make: chains with more or fewer beads, in longer or shorter lengths; or elements of 2, 3 or 4 cardboard rings, one within another, held together with large beads.

BEAD CHAIN SECTIONS

● Thread a piece of copper wire through a bead. Let about $\frac{3}{4}$ inch (2 cm) extend on each side of the bead (Drawing 1). Roll up the wire ends with round-nose pliers (Drawing 2).

● Do the same thing with 2 or 3 beads threaded on the same wire. Use a piece of wire longer than you did for a single bead.

● Link the bead groups together with S-shaped hooks. Make the hooks from pieces of florist's wire or hanger wire. Cut pieces about $1\frac{1}{2}$ inches (35 mm) long and bend them into "S" shapes with the round-nose pliers (Drawing 3).

● To join the sections together, open the "S" and hook the curve through the ring of the wire-and-bead unit. Close the "S" with pliers (Drawing 4).

Make several sections of different lengths in this way.

CIRCLE SECTIONS

● Using the cardboard bands you have prepared, make circles joined at the end with staples (Drawing 5) in sizes which fit together, one within another. You can paint the cardboard rings in similar shades, or paint each ring a different, interesting color.

● To join 2 or 3 of the rings, hold them together and make holes with a large needle through them all (Drawing 6). Thread a bead on a piece of copper wire. At one end of the wire make a tight loop to hold the bead in place. Thread the other end of the wire through the holes made with the needle, thread a second bead and end the wire with a loop (Drawing 7).

● Make 2 or more rings into a single unit by placing several rings between the enclosing beads (Drawing 8).

● Make many different elements by varying the size and number of the rings and the beads you use.

Join the chains and the circular sections using S-shaped hooks as described above.

To hang the garland, attach a nylon line to the end bead. Make several knots in the line and put a drop of white glue on the knots to keep the beads from slipping.

The drawing here is an example of a mobile made up of three garlands hung from an iron wire. You will need a heavier iron wire such as coat-hanger wire for the cross-bar of the mobile.

Attach the elements to the wire by tying them on and adding glue for extra strength.

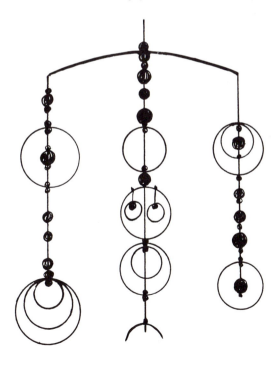

DECORATIVE PANELS

PANEL WITH RED BACKGROUND
(See the photo above.)

This design is inspired by an Indian painting from the state of Jalisco in Mexico.

Materials
● Sheet of drawing paper 20 x 26 inches (50 x 65 cm)

● Tubes of gouache paints

Procedure
● Enlarge the design shown in the photo, using the square transfer method found on page 95.

● Paint it with gouache paints in lively, luminous colors like the ones used here for the panel with birds. Work carefully and neatly for the best results.

Materials

● Beige color drawing paper, 20 x 26 inches (50 x 65 cm)

● Tracing paper and carbon paper

PANEL WITH BIRDS

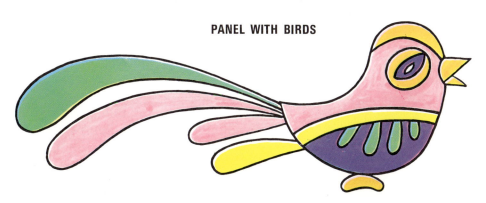

● Tube of thickish ink in deep green (sometimes used in wood-block printing)

● Tubes of gouache paints

● Thick and thin paintbrushes

● Dried-out ballpoint pen

Procedure

● Over the entire sheet of paper brush on the deep green color, diluted with water, to obtain a transparent shade which varies in light and dark tones. If you prefer you can dab the ink on with a small wad of cotton. Let dry.

● Enlarge on tracing paper the bird design shown half-size on page 21. Use the square transfer method shown on page 95.

● Use a sheet of carbon paper to reproduce the bird as many times as necessary by placing the carbon paper between the tracing paper and the drawing paper. Re-trace the outline with a dried-out ballpoint pen in each position.

● Decorate the spaces between the birds with small flowers.

● Paint the birds and flowers with thick gouache paints. Use bright, lively colors and finish off by outlining the figures with black lines.

FLOWERING TREE

(Shown in the color photo on page 13.)

This beautiful ornament immediately adds a Mexican feeling to a room.

Materials

● Sheets of metallic paper (1 side metallic, 1 side plain) in orange and red

● Sheets of double-face metal foils: gold-red, gold-silver, etc.

● Sheets of fluorescent-color paper: cherry, violet, hot pink, orange

● 9 large plastic foam balls, $1\frac{1}{2}$ inches (4 cm) in diameter

● Copper wire or flexible iron florist's wire

● Large sheets of flexible cardboard

● Narrow strip of wood 1 yard (about 1 metre) long, $1\frac{1}{2}$ inches (3 cm) wide and $\frac{1}{2}$ inch (1 cm) thick

● Wooden strips about $\frac{5}{8}$ inch (1.5 cm) wide and $\frac{1}{8}$–$\frac{1}{4}$-inch (3–5 mm) thick

● Gouache paints: white and hot pink

● Clay or plastic flowerpot with at least a 5-inch (12-cm) diameter

● Plaster of Paris

● Wooden spring-type clothespins

Construction

You are going to make a tree trunk, large leaf outlines for the tree, and glue on different-colored flowers.

TREE OUTLINE

● Prepare some plaster in a small plastic bowl, following the package directions. Stir well until it is the consistency of cream.

● Pour the plaster into the flowerpot and place the long wooden strip in the middle. Hold in place until the plaster hardens. This strip will form the central vertical trunk of the tree.

● Using the square transfer method (see page 95), enlarge the leaf patterns shown on page 23. There are five different shapes.

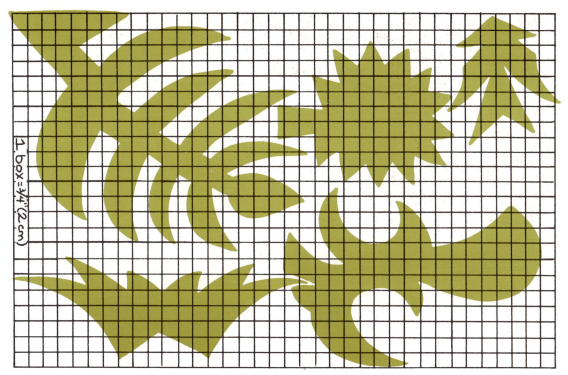

1 box = ¾" (2 cm)

Reproduce each twice on cardboard, except for the two shapes which form the top. You only need one of each of these.

● Cut them out and glue or staple them in place on the central trunk, following the photo for placement.

● To give the construction more strength, glue two of the small strips of wood to the backs of the leaves (Drawing 1).

● Prepare a mixture of the white and pink gouache paints in a cup. (Mix enough to paint the entire structure.)

● As shown in the photo you are following, paint the wood, cardboard leaves and the flowerpot with the mixed gouache colors. Let dry.

FLOWERS

The 9 large flowers are made from star shapes and circles cut from paper. The center of each is a plastic foam ball. You need 2 stars and 2 circles of decreasing size for each flower (if you use more layers the flowers will look even richer). The 2 small flowers are made the same way but without the ball in the middle.

● Freehand, cut stars from the metallic paper, with diameters of about 9 inches (22 cm).

● Cut stars with 6-inch (15-cm) diameters from the fluorescent paper, and circles with $2\frac{1}{2}$–$3\frac{1}{4}$-inch (6–8 cm) diameters.

● Cut circles with 5-inch (12-cm) dia-

meters from the double-face metal foil and fringe them all around.

● Paint the plastic balls bright pink.

● Glue together the middles of a large foil circle, a star of colored paper, a fringed circle in metal foil and a small paper circle, one on top of the others, varying the colors (Drawing 2).

● Pierce 2 holes in the middle with a large needle.

● Pass a piece of wire through one of the holes, then through the plastic foam ball and back through the other central hole (Drawing 3). Pull the wire tight in the back and twist closed. Cut off the excess (Drawing 4).

● Glue together the small flowers in the same way but without the plastic foam ball.

● Fold the fringes on the round metal circles towards the middle. Glue the different parts to the tree, holding them in place while the glue dries with spring clothespins (preferably wooden, since they will open wider).

Note: The tree will be quite heavy when assembled. If it is top-heavy and won't stand up, glue a large circle of wood to the bottom of the flowerpot to serve as a stand. Paint it the same color as the pot.

PAINTING ON CORK

(See the completed painting in the background of the picture on page 24.)

Materials
● A square of compressed cork, 12 inches (30 cm) in each direction. (These squares are made for cork walls, bulletin boards and insulation.) You can also use finely grained and tightly compressed corkboard.

● Gouache paints and cup or palette. With 5 tubes (turquoise blue, vermillion, lemon yellow, black and white) you can make all of the colors you'll need. The examples you see on these pages were painted with these colors.

● Tracing paper

● Very soft white pencil

Procedure
● The few Mexican designs shown on these pages are to provide inspiration. You can create your own or you can enlarge them. Lay them out according to your taste.

As always with **Mexican art, the colors you** use must be **very lively.**

● To enlarge the birds use the square-transfer method (see page 95) or a pantograph.

● On the cork panel draw a stylized bird with white pencil. Add flowers and scrolls around the bird figure.

● Mix several different colors of gouache separately in cups or on a palette. The paint must be thick. Paint on the cork following the white lines. Use good brushes shaped into neat points.

● Let the colors dry, then outline them with painted black lines.

Note: To reinforce the cork, which is very fragile, you can glue it onto a cardboard square of the same size. If you want to hang your work, just glue on a picture hanger.

MURAL PANEL

(See the design in color on page 27.)

Materials
● Drawing paper

● Soft-tip marking pens

● Tracing paper

● Beads, gilded cord or gilded twine for decoration (optional)

Procedure
● Reproduce the design on page 27 (or something similar, if you want to be creative) on tracing paper, enlarging as much as you want.

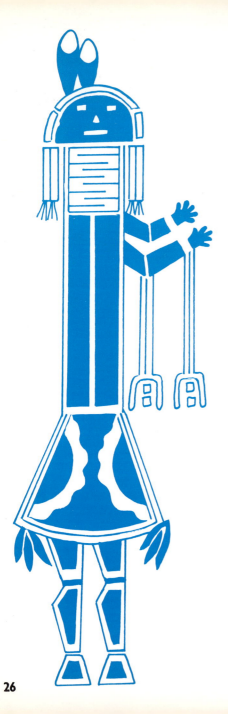

● Transfer the central design onto the drawing paper. Then transfer the outer pattern four times to form a complete circle.

● Color with soft-tip pens.

● If you like, glue small beads between the designs in the middle circle, and glue gilded cord or twine over the innermost circle of the design.

OTHER IDEAS

You can reproduce your design on a roll of painting paper to make a large mural which you can use to conceal a door or a part of a room from the guests at your festival.

● The same design can also be used to decorate a cloth napkin or cushion cover by embroidering it with colored wool on thick brown canvas.

● You can even decorate a tablecloth with this design by using decals of felt, which you transfer to the fabric by pressing a hot iron over the design.

PROGRAM

(Shown on the right in the color photo on page 75.)
On the left is an inventive design for the front of a menu or a program, inspired by ancient Mexican paintings.

The same design can be used to make small trays.

Materials

● Rectangle of black drawing paper 20 x 4 inches (50 x 10 cm)

● Tracing paper and soft white pencil or crayon

● Gouache paints

¼ of pattern

Procedure

● Fold the drawing paper into 2 equal parts to make a rectangle 10 x 4 inches (25 x 10 cm).

● Use tracing paper to trace your design on the left.

● Coat the back of the tracing paper with the white pencil or crayon.

● Place the tracing on the drawing paper and transfer the design by pressing hard along the outline with a dried-out ballpoint pen.

● Paint with bright gouache colors.

PIÑATAS

(Shown in color on page 13.)

In Mexico these large terra-cotta birds painted in lively colors are filled with little presents. Only by breaking the *piñatas* can children discover the treasures inside. We will make a much simpler *piñata* from glued paper over a bottle form with nothing inside and use it as a decorative object.

Materials

● 2 large plastic bottles from mineral water, bleach, etc. (Be sure you wash them out thoroughly.)

● Transparent tape

● Wallpaper paste (flour-and-water paste will also do)

● 24 sheets of newspaper

● Small bowl of water

● Workboard covered with waterproof plastic cloth

● White water-base paint

● Gouache paints

Construction

● Cut the 2 bottles into slices from the base to the neck (see Drawing 1).

● Put the slices in order as shown in Drawing 2, and hold them together with the tape. Note that one of the bottle tops is placed at the head of the bottle, tilted upwards more sharply than the bottle top at the other end, which is slipped into the body a little.

● Wrap up the bottles with a sheet of newspaper (Drawing 3), and hold the paper in place with tape.

● Mix the wallpaper paste following the directions on the package: it must be neither too thick nor too thin, just the consistency of heavy cream.

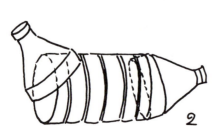

Tear the newspaper into long narrow strips and let them soak in the paste for half an hour.

When they are well soaked, take the strips one by one and cover the entire form with them. Add more strips at the head to make it look more like a bird head. Make the body very thick, giving the bird a large breast.

Let dry for several days. The pasted paper will harden and you will have a lovely papier-mâché *piñata* bird ready to decorate.

Decoration

Brush on a first coat of white water-base paint, as a primer.

When the first coat dries, decorate with gouache using bright colors.

If you want to hang the *piñata* bird, make a small hole in the middle of the back and push in a small screw eye coated with strong glue. A wire can go through the screw eye after it sets.

RED AND BLACK VASE

Materials
● Wide-necked plastic jar
● Water-base paints, black and red

Procedure
The decoration of this vase is made up simply of horizontal or vertical stripes and triangles, with the two colors alternating.

JARS WITH MEXICAN DECORATION

(See design in color on next page. Finished jar is in photo on page 12.)

Materials
● Plastic bottles in interesting shapes (wash them out)
● Soft black pencil
● Ballpoint pen
● Water-base paints
● Transparent tape

Procedure
● With a penknife, cut off the top of a bottle as neatly as possible, then straighten the edge with a pair of heavy all-purpose scissors. The cut jar should be about $5\frac{1}{2}$ inches (14 cm) high.

● Transfer the Mexican bird design shown on the next page onto a piece of tracing paper. Blacken the back with a soft pencil.

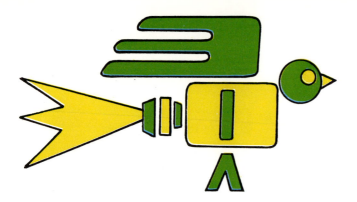

● Attach this tracing to the outside of the bottle with transparent tape.

● Trace the design onto the bottle with the ballpoint pen.

● Paint the design with a fine paintbrush using bright colors.

● Above and below the bird design decorate the jar with an imaginative pattern of triangles and stripes, as shown in above drawing.

CANDLEHOLDER

(Shown in photo on page 12.)

Materials
● Small glass jar (from seasonings or preserves, for example)

● Water-base paints, black and green

● Candle, the wider the better

Procedure
● Paint on the jar a design of stripes, rectangles, lines and boxes, some black and some green.

● Let a little melted wax drip into the bottom of the jar.

● Stand the candle in the melted wax. It will drip (unless dripless) into the empty areas of the jar.

BIRD PLACE-CARD

(Shown in the photo on page 12.)

Materials
● 2 rectangles of flexible cardboard

● Silver metallic paper or colored paper

● Crepe paper: bright green, turquoise, hot pink, golden yellow

● Transparent glue

Construction
● Cut out 2 cardboard shapes, following the pattern on the next page twice.

● Cut out 6 bands, $\frac{3}{4}$ x $7\frac{1}{4}$ inches (2 x 18 cm), from each color of crepe paper.

● Lay one bird form flat on a table and coat it with glue.

● Lay on the crepe paper bands, from the back, lining them up with the tail, over-lapping one over another. Those at the neck end must line up with the neck. When all the bands have been placed, add a little glue to hold them all well.

● Spread glue on the other cardboard piece and place it on top of the first, with its strips attached, making sure the outlines match perfectly. Be sure you don't get glue on the rectangular base shown in the shaded portion of the pattern.

● Cut out another copy of the pattern, this time using silver paper. Glue it over the cardboards. (You can instead paint directly over the cardboard with metallic silver paint.)

● Fold the 2 rectangular base flaps outwards (the shaded part of the pattern) to form a base for the bird.

● Write the guest's name on the body of the bird.

● With a knife or scissors lightly fringe the ends of some of the paper bands. You can also curl them by holding a point near the end of a band between your thumb and the knife or scissors' edge and pulling gently.

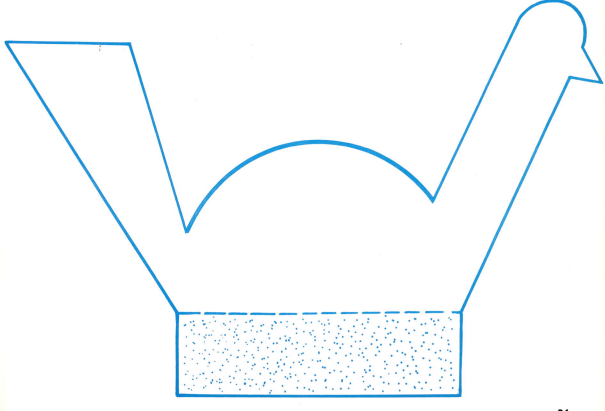

COSTUMES

Everyday Mexican costumes are easy to make using only simple, inexpensive materials and equipment.

For festive occasions women's hairstyles and jewelry are important parts of the costumes. You can wear beaded jewelry you might already own, or you can buy inexpensive glass beads and string them yourself in a design you like. You can even make your own beads out of metal foil.

METAL FOIL BEADS

● Cut small triangles of different sizes from metallic paper or foil.

● Roll them around a knitting needle, starting at the wide end.

● Tape the point down with a small strip of transparent tape.

The longer the triangle you cut, the thicker the bead will be.

● Simply string the "beads" on a piece of cord or thread.

In the same way, you can make multi-colored beads by cutting triangles out of gift-wrapping paper or colorful magazine pictures.

GIRL'S (*MUCHACHA'S*) EVERYDAY OUTFIT

This is a basic Mexican costume which is very easy to make. It includes:

● White cotton blouse with a low neckline, bordered with cross stitches.

You will need a white blouse or shirt (a tee-shirt will do). Cut out bands of crepe paper and on them draw rows of "cross stitches" with a soft-tip marking pen. Simply sew the crepe paper bands around the neckline and sleeves as shown in the drawing of the girl.

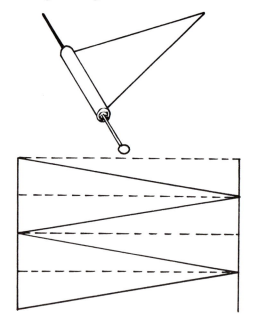

The skirt is made from a large rectangular piece of cloth. A belt will hold the folds (or pleats) in place. Let the folds show above the belt. Prepare a large crepe paper band with cross stitches drawn on it, and sew it onto the bottom of the skirt.

Light sandals or thongs.

The beautiful flowing scarf frequently worn by Mexican women, which goes especially well with this outfit, is called a *cabozo.* It is a long straight band of cotton (or silk) with full fringes at each end as much as 20 inches (50 cm) long. You can make the *cabozo* from soft, supple fabric and add crepe paper fringes. For a fancier look, use beads strung on cotton thread for the fringes.

BOY'S (*MUCHACHO'S*) EVERYDAY OUTFIT

Plain-colored, long-sleeved shirt with open collar.

White or light-colored pants.

● Large brightly colored blanket. This essential Mexican garment is called a *sarape*. Mexican men and boys wrap themselves up in it for protection from the cold or from bad weather. They carry it folded over their shoulders. You can use a large piece of striped fabric instead of a blanket. Attach wool fringes to the ends.

● Espadrilles (canvas shoes with flexible soles).

● Straw hat, preferably with a wide brim. You can make your own Mexican hat by following the instructions on page 35.

TRADITIONAL MEXICAN MAN'S COSTUME

You can make the traditional costume shown in color here with:

● White pajamas or judo outfit. (If you don't have this to start with, use a white shirt with long sleeves and an open collar, and a pair of blue-jeans with the legs rolled up to the calf.)

● Wide leather belt.

● A *poncho* called a *jorongo* to be worn

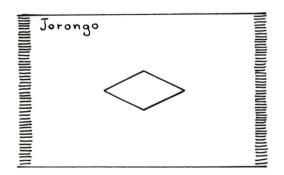

Jorongo

over the shirt and pants. The smaller version of this *poncho* is called a *gaban*. It's a big woollen rectangle with a hole cut in the middle for the head to pass through. (You don't have to make this garment from woollen fabric. You can make a very handsome *poncho* from crepe paper by glueing brightly colored strips of crepe paper onto any solid-color fabric. The fringes are also made of crepe paper, stapled or glued on.)

● Sandals with straps wrapped around

the foot as shown in the picture, or else plastic beach sandals (thongs).

● The hat, or *sombrero,* is the most famous part of a traditional Mexican costume, and the trickiest part of the outfit for you to make.

MEXICAN HAT (*SOMBRERO*)

Materials

● 2 large sheets of cardboard, oaktag or Bristol board, about 20 inches x 26 inches (50 cm x 65 cm)

● White glue

● Stapler and knife or X-Acto blade in holder

● Wooden or metal straightedge with a hole at one end

● Compass, for drawing circles (optional)

● Large thumbtack or pushpin

● Paints, water-base

● Large board, soft enough so you can push in a thumbtack or pushpin

Construction

● Place a sheet of cardboard on the large board.

● If you have a compass, place the point in the center of the cardboard 2 inches (5 cm) from the top edge. If not, pass the point of a thumbtack through the hole in the straightedge and into the board in the same spot.

● With the compass or using the straightedge as a guide as shown in Drawing 1, you will draw two circular lines.

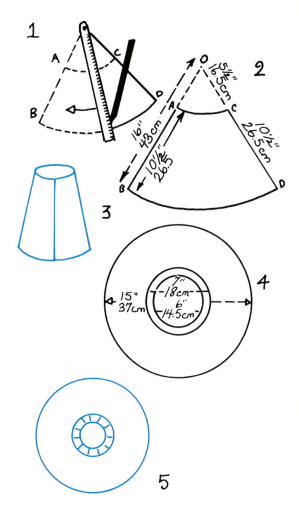

● Draw the first line at a distance of 5½ inches (14 cm) from the middle (from A to C in Drawing 2).

● Next draw a line an additional 10½ inches (26.5 cm) from the middle (from B to D in Drawing 2).

● Draw lines connecting A to B and C to D and cut out the figure you have drawn.

● To make the cone-shaped central part of the hat, roll up the cut-out shape, overlap the edge $\frac{1}{2}$ inch (1.3 cm) and staple it closed (see Drawing 3).

● Using your compass or the straightedge and thumbtack method described above, draw on the other piece of cardboard:

● A circle with a 15-inch (38-cm) diameter.

● Another circle inside the first with a 7-inch (18-cm) diameter.

● One more inside circle with a 6-inch (14.5-cm) diameter (see Drawing 4).

● Cut out with the point of a knife or an X-Acto blade the central (smallest) circle.

● Draw tabs between the inner and middle circles as shown in Drawing 5, $\frac{1}{2}$ inch (1.3 cm) apart, and cut them out with scissors.

● Push the tabs up at right angles and coat their outside edges with glue.

● Glue the circle with the tabs turned up inside the central cone-shaped piece as shown in Drawing 6.

● Cut two strips of cardboard, $24\frac{1}{2}$ inches (61 cm) long and $3\frac{1}{2}$ inches (9 cm) wide. Overlap the ends $\frac{1}{2}$ inch (1.3 cm) and staple them together (see Drawing 7).

● Draw a pencil line all along the edge of the band, $\frac{3}{4}$ inch (2 cm) from the bottom. Cut tabs up to this line, $\frac{1}{2}$ inch (1.3 cm) apart.

● Staple the two new ends of the band together. Push the tabs up at right angles and coat the inside edges with glue.

● Place the central construction on top of

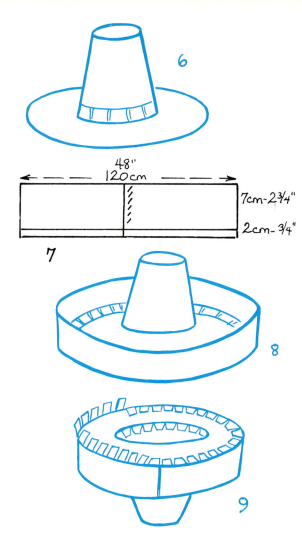

the tabs as shown in Drawing 8 and press down on the edge firmly with your fingers. Drawing 9 shows the hat turned upside-down.

● Paint your *sombrero* with bright colors in a pattern of stripes and triangles as shown in the color photo on page 34.

GIRL'S FESTIVE HAIRSTYLES

COIFFURE (HAIRSTYLE) NO. 1

(Shown in color on the right side of page 39.)

This style is inspired by a hairstyle worn at a wedding in the state of Oaxaca (pronounced wha ha' ka).

Materials

● Strong hair clips

● Hairpins

● 7 pieces of decorative paper (color pages from magazines or gift-wrapping paper) about 6 x 13 inches (15 x 32 cm)

● Ball of black wool (which can be re-used): also one each in blue and orange

● 7 wooden or plastic beads

● Transparent tape

Procedure

● Make a long roll by taking a piece of the decorative paper and rolling it tightly around a knitting needle, beginning at a corner (Drawing 1). Finish by taping the end of the roll shut with a piece of transparent tape (Drawing 2). The finished roll should be about 12 inches (30 cm) long. Make 7 rolls.

● Thread a wooden bead on each roll and glue it in place one-third of the way down (Drawing 3).

● Unroll the blue and red wool balls and wind them into skeins 20 inches (50 cm) long, which will make strands 40 inches (1 m) long when cut once.

● Put the two colors together in one big bunch and divide the entire thing into three parts.

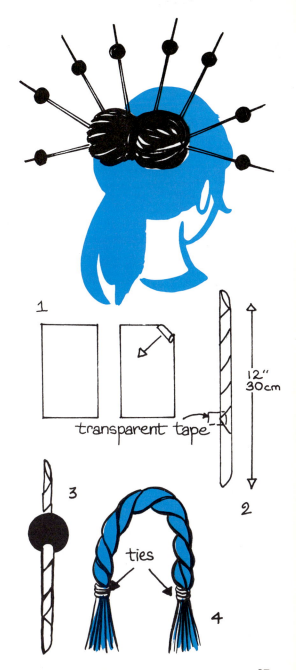

1

transparent tape

12"
30cm

2

3

ties

4

● Braid the middle section of the strands only. Tie off the braid when it reaches from ear to ear (Drawing 4).

● Gather your hair together in a pony tail. Place the pony tail on top of your head and hold it in place with 2 hairpins.

● Attach the ball of black wool to the back of your head securely, using hairpins and clips.

● Stick the paper rolls into the ball of yarn. To keep them steady, hold them with some clips. (See color picture.)

● Wear hoop earrings.

● Around your neck wear a long necklace of small beads, in several strands if you like (not shown).

COIFFURE NO. 2

Materials

● 6 rolls of crepe paper in 3 different colors (green, black and pink, for example), each about 2½ inches (6 cm) wide

● 2 packages of small plastic foam balls

● Tube of transparent glue

● Nylon thread

● Hairpins and clips

Procedure

● If your crepe paper is very wide, cut it into ribbons, 2½ inches (6 cm) wide, each the entire length of the roll.

● Take 2 bands of each color. Fold them in half to find the middle point.

● Braid the central section together to make a 14-inch (35-cm) length. The braided section must reach from just above the right ear to just above the left ear. Tie off the beginning and end of the braided section with nylon thread.

● At the ends of the strips, which can vary in length from 8–16 inches (20–40 cm), glue on plastic foam balls. To do this, place the braids on a table and spread out the end strips. Place a little glue on each plastic foam ball and put it in place on a strip. Wait until the glue is completely dry before placing the braid on your head.

This hairstyle is held in place with hairpins and clips. Do not wear a necklace with this style.

COIFFURE NO. 3

(Shown in color at left on page 39.)

Materials

● Roll of crepe paper

● 3 cardboard circles, 6 inches (15 cm) in diameter

● 2 long rolls of paper, as you made for style No. 1

Back

● Elastic bands

● Glue

● Small ball of blue yarn

● Soft-tip marking pens

● Hairpins and clips

Procedure

● Decorate the 3 cardboard circles with soft-tip marking pens (for design ideas see the color illustration on page 39).

● Make a thick twisted band from the crepe paper which you first cut in strips $2\frac{1}{2}$–$3\frac{1}{4}$ inches (6–8 cm) wide. (You will need 6–9 strips.) The twisted band must be about 16 inches (40 cm) long. Tie off the ends with small elastic bands.

● Cut 80 strands of wool 20 inches (50 cm) long.

● Slip 40 strands into each elastic band, carefully spreading them to hide completely the ends of the crepe-paper twist.

● Glue the 3 cardboard circles to the back of the twist as shown on page 39.

● Attach a plastic foam ball to one end of each paper roll. Stick the other end between the braided bands (or glue in place).

● Hold the assembly on your head using hairpins or clips. Do not wear a necklace with this hairstyle.

DRESSES

To complement the girl's festive hairstyles, here are several dresses which you can make using everyday equipment and materials you can easily find.

These different costumes can be made from whatever fabric you have on hand or from inexpensive materials like felt or crepe paper. You can use several sheets of crepe paper to give you the required width, joining them with wide strips of masking tape. Two-layer crepe paper is available and is best for durability. (Be sure to check that it is flameproof.)

It is not possible to give exact measurements for the costumes since they must vary based on the sizes and shapes of the children or adults who will wear them. The measurements given here should serve as guidelines, and the patterns are simple enough so that anyone can adapt them.

GIRL'S COSTUME NO. 1

(See the drawing on page 41.)

This costume is made up of a long tunic worn over an ankle-length, gathered or pleated skirt, preferably in contrasting colors. Wear it with Coiffure No. 3 (page 38).

Materials

● Felt or crepe paper in lemon yellow for the tunic, deep blue or red for the skirt

● Glue (UHU Glue Stick is suitable for crepe paper and white glue for felt)

● Roll of masking tape

● Nylon thread

● Stapler

● Soft-tip marking pens in different colors

Construction

TUNIC

● Measure the wearer, and cut the pattern for the tunic (Drawing 1) from the material

A

B

1

2

you have chosen. The tunic should reach to a little below the knees. Note that the pattern shown is only half the depth you will need—the upper dotted line indicates the shoulder line.

● In the middle make an opening, slightly rounded and dipping in the front.

● Make a cut down the middle of the back, from A to B in the pattern, to allow the head to pass through easily. You can sew on a snap fastener at the back of the neck.

● Decorate either with soft-tip marking pens or by glueing on strips of colored paper.

● Staple the sides closed, leaving about 9 inches (23 cm) open on each side for armholes.

SKIRT

You can use a long skirt if you have one, or make one from a rectangle of felt 32 x 80 inches (80 cm x 2 m). You can also make a skirt from crepe paper. You will have to join 2 rolls of paper together to make it the necessary depth. Join them by laying the 2 rolls out flat on a table or on the floor, match the edges exactly, and lay a strip of masking tape over the seam on the back (Drawing 2 on page 41).

Pass a gathering thread through the length of the skirt waist. Bring the two edges together and staple them closed, starting from the bottom, and leaving an opening at the top large enough to easily slip on the skirt (Drawing 2). Push the gathers together at the waist.

GIRL'S COSTUME NO. 2

(Shown in color on page 43.)

This graceful costume is very easy to make.

Recommended hairstyle: 2 long braids (your own hair or dark wool) tied with large, bright ribbons.

Materials

● Crepe paper or fabric used for linings: white, deep blue and light blue

● Roll of white paper

● Roll of masking tape

● Stapler

● Soft-tip marking pens

Construction

SKIRT

● To make it in crepe paper, cut lengthwise bands from rolls of crepe paper, each band 8 inches (20 cm) wide in decreasing lengths. As shown in Drawing 1, depending on the

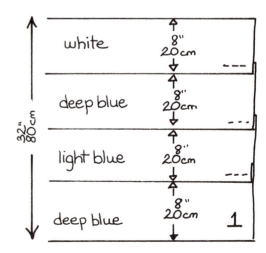

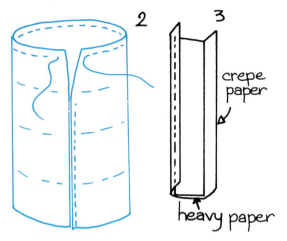

crepe paper

heavy paper

depth required, glue together 4 or 5 bands, alternating colors. Each band should overlap the one before it slightly. Begin glueing with the bottom band.

● Staple together the sides. Leave an opening at the top back so the skirt can be easily slipped on and off.

● Pass a gathering thread through the waist and tie the ends together (Drawing 2).

● Conceal the waist with a belt made of heavy paper covered with crepe paper (Drawing 3).

If you are using fabric, proceed in the same way, but assemble the horizontal bands on a sewing machine.

PONCHO

You can use a real *poncho* if you already own one. If not, make one from fabric (or heavy white paper) and decorate it with soft-tip marking pens using a design inspired by the illustration on page 43.

● Make 2 bands, each 16 x 32 inches (40 x 80 cm). Glue or sew them together as shown in Drawing 4.

● Add crepe paper fringes all around the bottom edges.

Under the *poncho* wear a brightly colored blouse or tee-shirt.

Wear espadrilles or sandals on your feet.

GIRL'S COSTUME NO. 3

(Shown in color on page 46.)

The long skirt, very wide and very deeply pleated, adds character to this costume.

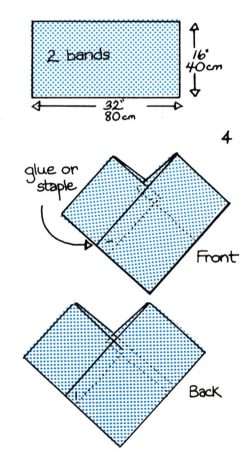

Wear your hair pulled back with a large ribbon at the nape of the neck.

Materials

- 4 rolls of red crepe paper
- Plain white paper
- Soft-tip marking pens, pink and green
- White glue
- Roll of wide masking tape
- Stapler

Construction

SKIRT

- Glue the 4 rolls of crepe paper together to form a rectangle which is deep enough to reach from your waist to your feet, and long enough to form a full skirt.

- Prepare a band of white paper 8 inches (20 cm) wide and long enough to fit around the skirt near the bottom edge (if necessary, glue together several sheets of paper end to end).

- Decorate the white paper with a design like the one shown on page 46, using soft-tip marking pens.

- Glue this band 8 inches (20 cm) from the bottom edge of the skirt.

- Cut deep fringes into the part of the skirt which extends below the white band.

- Pass a gathering thread through the length of the skirt waist.

- Staple the sides together to make the skirt, leaving an opening so the skirt can be slipped on and off easily.

- Fold the pleats and adjust at the waist.

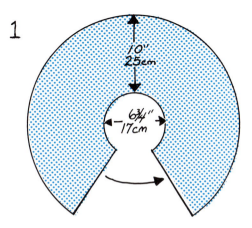

1

Conceal the waist with a band of crepe paper, folded in three.

COLLAR

The collar is made from white paper decorated with soft-tip marking pens.

- Cut out a circular pattern as shown in Drawing 1, with a width of 10 inches (25 cm).

- Decorate with the same pattern used on the skirt band.

- Place the collar around the neck and staple the two ends together at the back.

Under the collar wear a short-sleeved blouse or tee-shirt the same color as the skirt.

INDIAN DANCER OF SAN MIGUEL

(Shown in color on page 47.)

Materials

- Satinette, felt, or crepe paper
- Glue

- Roll of masking tape
- Stapler
- Wooden beads
- White and colored paper
- Soft-tip marking pens
- Small bedsheet
- Plastic foam balls

Construction

This costume is worn over a tee-shirt or short-sleeved shirt and bathing trunks.

TUNIC

- This is made simply of 2 rectangles of plain cloth, preferably white, sewn together at the shoulders. It should reach down to mid-thigh. You can, if necessary, use 2 bath towels of the same color.

- The decorations are made with bands or designs cut from crepe paper and sewn in place with large stitches. For design ideas see the illustration at the right.

- At the waist wear a belt made from a band of crepe paper folded in three.

CAPE

- This is a small bedsheet trimmed with colorful crepe-paper bands. You can also make the cape from crepe-paper sheets glued together side by side.

- Fasten the cape on the chest with the flaps thrown over the shoulders.

JEWELRY AND ORNAMENTS

- The wide wristbands are made from bands of thin cardboard 4 inches (10 cm)

wristband

1

headband

2

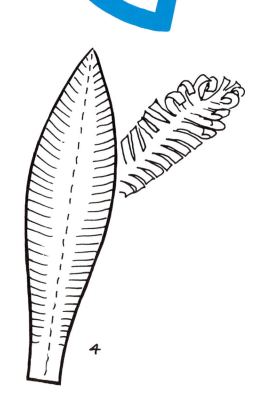

3

wide, decorated with colorful paper cutouts (Drawing 2).

● The leg ornaments are also made of cardboard cut out following the shape of Drawing 3. They should be between 8–12 inches (20–30 cm) high depending on the size of the wearer. The wristbands and leg ornaments are put together directly on the wearer with transparent tape.

● You can make a large collar for the cape using plastic foam balls or "metal" beads (make as shown on page 32).

● Complete the accessories with ankle bracelets of beads or plastic foam balls.

HEAD-DRESS

Make a headband from thin cardboard and decorate it with beads or small bits of colorful paper glued on (Drawing 1).

The feathers are cut out of white paper:

● From a rectangular piece of stiff paper 4 to 5 inches (10 to 12 cm) wide and 10 to 12 inches (25 to 30 cm) tall, cut out the feather shape shown in Drawing 4.

● Use scissors to fringe the feather on either side of the middle line and curl the fringes between your thumb and one blade of the scissor.

Prepare 5 or 6 feathers and staple them to the back of the headband. On your feet wear leather sandals with thongs.

4

GAMES

Here are some fanciful games which have Mexican themes.

Some of these games, particularly the more physically active ones, will appeal to a party of older youngsters and help to liven up a Mexican festival. Of course these can, like the other games described here, be played by younger children, as long as the difficulty of the tests is modified to reflect the age of the players.

HOUSE PARTY

Game of Skill and Action

Number of players: from 1 to 7.

Hilly playing area.

Materials

● Chairs, benches, hoops, logs, and so on.

● Basket (an Easter egg basket, for instance, that will fit on the head)

Preparation for the Game

Prepare an obstacle course which requires the players, for example, to:

walk a straight line drawn on the ground,

climb onto a chair,

cross a bench in 4 steps,

crouch and waddle like a duck for 10 feet (3 m),

pick up a hoop and walk through it,

walk across a path of logs set on the ground, and so forth.

You can add many other obstacles depending on the kind of terrain you have.

RULES OF THE GAME

● Señor Alligator, the master of the house, gives a basket to player No. 1 and explains the rules of the game. He then sits in a chair placed so that he can see all of the developments in the contest.

● He signals to the player, who stands at the starting line and places the basket on his head.

● At a signal from Señor Alligator the player starts the obstacle course. He must do all of the required activities as quickly as possible, but without letting the basket fall.

● If he succeeds, he must bring the basket back to Señor Alligator, who gives him a reward.

● If the player drops the basket, he is eliminated and the next contestant takes his place at the starting line.

● Use a watch with a second hand to time each successful contestant and then give a prize only to the one or two who have completed the course in the shortest time.

TREASURE OF THE AZTECS

Terrific Outdoor Game

Number of players: from 4 to 12.

Hilly wooded playing area.

Materials

● Small cotton bag with 3 plastic balls in it, and 3 extra balls

● Brightly colored crepe paper strips

Preparation for the Game

Mark off the limits of the playing area by attaching crepe paper strips to trees, making a field of about 240 square yards (200 m²).

RULES OF THE GAME

● The leader divides the players into 2 equal teams, the "Aztecs" and the "Feathered Serpents."

● Decide by lot which player receives the bag containing the "treasure."

● Without the knowledge of the other players, the chosen player hides the bag in a carefully chosen spot within the playing area. He must remember this spot exactly.

● He returns to the group and tells a fantastic story about Mexico, about the vegetation, for example. In telling this farfetched story the player must work in hidden clues to the location of the treasure, trying to give hints his own team will understand. Set a 2-minute time limit on the story.

Of course, the players from the other team will also be trying to understand the clues.

● At the end of the story, the leader of the game gives a signal and the 2 teams set out to find the "treasure."

● If the player who hid the treasure is a member of the Aztec team and the player who finds the treasure is an Aztec, the game leader adds a ball to the treasure and the Aztec team gets 4 points.

If a player from the Feathered Serpent team finds the treasure, the leader removes a ball from the bag and his team gets 2 points.

● When 2 players from opposing teams find the treasure at the same time, each team gets 2 points.

● The leader gets the group back together and a new round begins. Now it's the turn of a Feathered Serpent team member to hide the treasure.

● You can agree in advance on the number of rounds to be played. At the end of the last round, each team adds up its points.

● The leader must be sure not to forget to add or take away a ball, depending upon who wins each round.

● When the last ball must be removed from the bag, the game is over and the points are added up. You can then start another round from the beginning, with 3 balls.

PIÑATAS

Game of Skill and Action

Unlimited number of players (each round will have 2 players at a time). **2 leaders.**

Indoors (game room with a crossbeam) **or outdoors** (with a tree branch to use as a crossbar).

Materials

● 2 *piñatas*

● 11 yards (10 m) of twine

● 2 sticks, each 20 inches (50 cm) long

● 2 blindfolds

● 1 barrier, such as a ladder on its side or a convenient fence

Preparation for the Game

● Make the *piñatas* of pasted paper (see directions on page 28).

● Pass a thick rope several yards (metres) long through the screw eye attached to the middle of the back of the *piñata.*

● Pass the rope over the crossbeam or tree branch (later protect the branch with a small piece of plastic). The leader must be able to raise and lower the *piñatas* easily.

● Place the barrier about 2 yards (1.8 m) from the crossbar. The competitors stand behind the barrier.

RULES OF THE GAME

● One leader holds the 2 ropes in his hands.

● The competitors stand in place.

● A second leader blindfolds the competitors' eyes and hands them each a stick.

● At a signal from the second leader, the first leader raises and lowers the *piñatas* without stopping. The players must try to hit them with their sticks in passing.

If a competitor touches the rope he receives

a 1 point penalty. On the other hand, if he touches the *piñata* he is awarded 5 points. The second leader keeps score.

● The first player to get 15 points is the winner of the round. Then the next 2 players take a turn.

MAITRE D'HOTEL RODEO

Game of Skill and Action

Players: 10–12 years old, 8 players.

Outdoors, in an open space.

Materials

● 10 plastic or paper plates

● 10 plastic or paper cups

● 2 paper tablecloths

● 1 large board

● 2 sawhorses

Preparation for the Game

● Find an area free of obstructions for the rodeo.

● At one end of the field place 2 stools.

● On each of these place 5 cups, 5 plates, and 1 tablecloth.

● 11 yards (10 m) away place the saw-horses with the board resting on top to make a table.

RULES OF THE GAME

● The players are broken up into 2 teams of 4 players each.

● Two players from each team stand near the stools, each team near its own players.

● At the starting signal given by the game leader, the horseman: jumps on his horse (a stronger, heavier team mate), grabs a tablecloth and, with the "horse" galloping, places the tablecloth on the table, returns galloping to pick up, in groups, the plates and the cups and arranges them correctly on the table. In all, this requires 3 trips.

● If anything falls, the horseman must get down from his mount, pick up the fallen object and return to the starting line (that is, to the stool) to get back on his "horse."

● The other 2 players of each team (horse and rider) will relieve the first team when they are finished but return the objects from the table to the stool. The idea is, clearly, to do everything without either the rider or the object falling.

● The first team which has returned everything to its place wins.

You can make the game harder by putting water in the cups and pebbles on the plates.

THE TREASURE OF RAFAEL

Game of Stop-and-Go Action

Players: minimum of 10; boys and girls from 8 to 10 years of age.

Outdoors or game room.

Materials

● Scarf

● Pebbles (enough for 1 per person minus 1)

Story for the Game

Rafael has a treasure of precious stones (small pebbles in a knotted scarf). But it was stolen from him by Miguel and his robber band.

RULES OF THE GAME

● A player is chosen (by lot) to be Rafael. He leaves the game area.

● Secretly the other players choose one of the robbers to be Miguel.

● Miguel and his band stand in a circle, and pass the "treasure" around. Rafael stands outside the circle, with his back to the other players.

● When Rafael claps his hands, he turns around. The players squat down quickly, crossing their arms to hide the "treasure."

● Rafael tries to figure out who is holding the treasure and points to the player he suspects.

● If he is right, he takes a pebble from the treasure and keeps it. The player who was caught is eliminated.

● Another round begins the same way. Rafael has the right to as many rounds as there are players in the circle.

● If, after this number of attempts, Rafael has recovered more than half the pebbles of "treasure," he has won. If not, he loses to Miguel and his band.

Note: If Rafael chooses Miguel and he has the treasure, Rafael recovers it all and wins. Another round can then be played with new players as Miguel and Rafael.

THE EYE OF THE GREAT MAYA

Number of players: unlimited. In teams of 4.

Outdoors or indoors, with a wall at least 3 feet (1 m) tall to serve as a support for the gameboards.

Materials

● Bench

● Thick cardboard

● Black construction paper

● 5 cardboard boxes (shoeboxes, for example)

● Compass for drawing circles, scissors

● Soft-tip marking pen, straightedge

● Thumbtacks or pushpins

A Game of Observation and Action

Preparation for the Game

● On 2 squares of cardboard $10\frac{1}{2}$ inches (28 cm) per side, use a straightedge to draw parallel lines spaced $1\frac{1}{2}$ inches (4 cm) apart horizontally and vertically, dividing each cardboard into 49 boxes altogether.

● On a dozen small squares of cardboard $3\frac{1}{2}$ inches (9 cm) on each side, draw the same number of boxes. They will be $\frac{1}{2}$ inch (1.5 cm) square each.

● On the construction paper draw, then cut out:

9 circles with $1\frac{1}{2}$ inch (4 cm) diameters,

9 circles with 1 inch (3 cm) diameters,

9 circles with $\frac{3}{4}$ inch (2 cm) diameters,

40 circles with $\frac{1}{2}$ inch (1.5 cm) diameters,

40 circles with $\frac{3}{8}$ inch (12 mm) diameters,

40 circles with $\frac{1}{4}$ inch (10 mm) diameters.

● Place the 27 larger circles in the top of a shoebox with the thumbtacks.

● Divide the remaining 120 circles equally into the other 4 shoeboxes.

RULES OF THE GAME

● Place a bench against a wall and lean the 2 large ruled-off cardboards against the wall facing away from the players.

● 4 players sit in costume about 7 feet (2 m) from the wall.

● The leader gives each player 2 small cardboard squares and a box of small circles.

● While hidden from the players, the leader uses thumbtacks to stick the large circles to the boards: 3 large black circles, 3 medium-sized circles and 3 small circles. Then he turns the boards around to face the players.

● He lets the players study the boards for 2 minutes, then turns them around again to face the wall.

● At a signal from the leader, the players rummage through their boxes and try to place the circles on their boards in the same pattern as on the large boards.

● At the leader's signal the contestants stop, cross their arms and wait till he turns the large cards around again.

● The winner is the one who has placed all of the circles on his board correctly. He or she receives a nice prize. The player who has only one box right has the privilege of trying again in the next round.

Anyone who has not completed his board is eliminated.

A MEXICAN DANCE

Here is a dance which is typically Mexican and easy to perform. A Mexican melody for your dancing pleasure is provided on page 56. First master the individual steps, then you can put them together in a lively native dance.

THE *RASPA*

Literally *raspa* means "file" or "rasp." The movement of the arms in the first part symbolizes the back-and-forth motion of this tool.

The Steps

CHIBRELI (RASPA) STEP
●Hop onto your left foot, kicking out your right foot, keeping the right leg straight (Drawing 1). Your left arm is pulled in and your right arm is extended.

● Reverse your position, hopping onto your right foot and kicking out your left (Drawing 2), left arm extended, right arm pulled in.

The step is usually done with the man and woman facing each other, holding hands as shown in the drawings.

HOP STEP
● Put down your left foot and hop on it immediately. Put down your right foot.

Formation
The dancers stand in a double circle, the boys inside with their backs to the middle and the girls outside facing in.

At the beginning of the dance the boys and girls hold each other's hands at shoulder height.

introduction

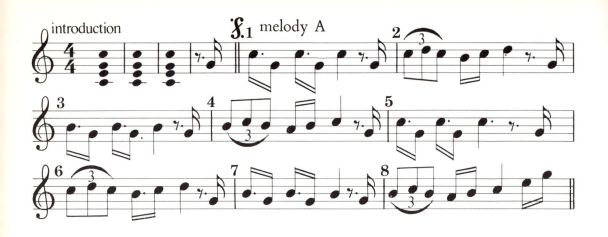

melody A

melody B

Description of the Dance

INTRODUCTION: 3 CHORDS

MELODY A: (in 4/4 time).

Measures 1–2. Leading off with the left foot, boys and girls execute 3 *chibreli* steps, followed by a full stop.

Measures 3–4: Begin again, starting this time with the right foot.

Measures 5–8 and following: Repeat the sequence 3 times.

MELODY B: (in 6/8 time).

Measures 1–2: The partners link their right arms and in 7 hops turn around once or twice in a clockwise direction. On the 8th hop they unlock elbows and clap hands.

Measures 3–4: Begin again, this time linking left elbows and moving in a counter-clockwise direction.

Measures 5–8: Repeat measures 1–4.

Repeat 3 times each melody and end the dance with a final repeat of A.

A STORY TO READ OR ACT OUT

Here is a beautiful story inspired by a Mexican legend which explains the origin of two Mexican volcanoes.

You may choose to tell this story in your own words, read it, or even better, act it out. Here you will find ideas for the setting, costumes and action of the story.

The story calls for 3 main characters: the *King,* the *Princess* and *Popocatepetl,* the captain. You can add as many *guards, servants* or *attendants* to the Princess as you wish, and even *dancers* if you want a large cast.

You can present this story in many ways. To avoid memorizing lines, you can have a narrator read the text of the story while actors perform the story wordlessly, in pantomime. If you prefer, you can make up dialogue for the characters and have them speak their lines, with the narrator filling in the background of the story.

Arrange for records of Mexican music, especially a song with an Indian flute, to serve as background music.

Scenery

● At the back of the scene arrange 3 or 4 columns of empty cardboard boxes piled one on top of another.

Cover them with brown paper and paint them with water-base paints in large Mexican designs like those used in the projects in this book.

● In front of the scenery at the right prepare a throne for the King, preferably on a raised platform, and 2 lower seats for the Princess and a servant.

These seats are made with a chair and two footstools covered with fabric decorated with designs made from paper and glued or stapled in place.

● At the right, set up a low bed made from 2 or 3 benches placed side by side.

Cover the benches with real or artificial fur, or with a dark cover decorated with paper cut-out designs.

Add some many-colored cushions on the bed.

● Complete the scene with some green plants and a few of the objects described in the section on decorations and scenery (page 14) such as decorative garlands or large painted panels. In addition, arrange for a good lighting set-up.

Costumes

The time period of this legend is so remote that the costumes can be extremely imaginative. It is not worthwhile to try for authentic costumes to portray legendary characters. You can draw your inspiration from the following ideas.

● *The King* can be dressed like the dancer of San Miguel shown on page 47, with additional golden ornaments.

● *The Captain* is dressed in the same style but with simple, colorful ornaments and without a cape. He carries a cardboard quiver and some arrows and holds a simple bow in his hand.

● *The Princess* wears a long tunic and many jewels, a beautiful hairstyle with a "bun" in the back if possible, and a long scarf.

● *Her attendants* are dressed in the same way but with less jewelry.

● *The guards and servants* wear short tunics with wide belts. The guards carry lances made from long sticks with spear points cut from cardboard and covered with aluminum attached at the tops. Below the point add a bunch of crepe-paper ribbons in bright colors.

THE LEGEND OF POPOCATEPETL

The Mexican people have an ancient legend which explains the birth of 2 great volcanoes in the southeast of their country. One is named Iztaechualt, which means "the volcano of the sleeping woman." Nearby is the volcano Popocatepetl, which even now can sometimes be seen glowing brightly in the evening sky.

The legend tells us that many years ago, before the mountains we know today even existed, the land was ruled by a King who was very rich and powerful, but very greedy as well. He had a magnificent palace, great riches, a beautiful daughter and a strong, loyal army. But he was not satisfied.

A brave young army officer named Popocatepetl loved the King's beautiful daughter, but he could not tell her. Even in those ancient times, a captain, no matter how brave, did not marry a princess.

One day the King invited all of his subjects to a great ball at the palace. There was

dancing and singing and everyone was happy. The beautiful Princess saw the handsome Popocatepetl gazing at her, and she smiled at him. This gave the young man courage, and he went to the King, fell on his knees, and declared his love for Princess Izia.

The King listened silently as the captain asked for permission to marry the Princess. The King saw the chance to gain more territory by sending the captain on a nearly impossible mission. Without even asking his daughter about her feelings, he made the brave soldier a promise.

The most powerful enemy of the King lived on the frontier of the kingdom. He had a powerful army, feared by everyone. No one had dared to challenge him. The King told Popocatepetl to take his soldiers and defeat this fearful enemy: if he was successful, he would marry the Princess.

The young captain was so deeply in love that he agreed to go into battle against the nearly unbeatable enemy. When they were left alone, the Princess took off her scarf, kissed it and gave it to Popocatepetl, promising to remain loyal to him until her death. He took the scarf and courageously left for battle.

Weeks passed, and Popocatepetl did not return. The Princess waited and waited for him, spending hours watching the road leading from the battlefield. Her companions tried to distract her with songs and dances, but she could not forget the dangers which the brave captain faced to win her.

The time came when the Princess did not have the courage to watch the road any longer. She lay on her bed, refusing to take the food which was brought to her.

The King heard of his daughter's actions and went to see her. When she asked for news of Popocatepetl, the King told her that all of his warriors had been killed in a fierce battle in the northern frontier. The Princess cried that, if her beloved captain was dead, she had nothing left to live for. She lay back, shut her eyes, and never opened them again.

The King understood then that, wishing to serve his greed, he had broken his daughter's heart.

Suddenly, loud cries came from outside the palace. They were victory cries! Popocatepetl, after defeating the terrible enemy, was returning home to the cheers of the crowd.

The happy soldier, still covered with dust from his long journey, hurried into the palace. He went to the King and reminded him of his promise of marriage. With great sorrow, the King told Popocatepetl that his daughter had died of a broken heart.

The grief-stricken captain was taken to the Princess' deathbed, where he wept, broke his arrows and sword and promised never to leave her side. He called his soldiers together and had them build a tomb, as tall as a mountain, for the Princess Izia. When the last stone was in place he took the Princess in his arms, climbed the mountain which would serve as her tomb and placed her at the top, near the sky. He lit a candle and began a solemn watch over the dead girl, promising to guard her forever.

This candle is the flame of the volcano Popocatepetl, which still reddens the skies of the Mexican night, guarding over the volcano of the sleeping woman, Iztaechualt.

★   ★

There are many dramatic and interesting scenes in this story which make it fun to act out. You only have to build one set, since all of the action takes place within the palace. To give your play an exciting finale, you can put on the final scene, where Popocatepetl places his Princess at the top of the mountain, as shadow-theatre:

● At the left side of the stage, between 2 of the columns, hang a white sheet which will serve as the shadow-theatre screen for the final scene.

● Behind this sheet place a long table for laying out the dead Princess and, at one side, a stool for the captain. Hide all of this by making a cardboard cutout to represent the silhouette of a pedestal and steps (see the drawing and the effect on page 63). The cardboard shape is placed just behind the sheet.

● Place a spotlight about $6\frac{1}{2}$ feet (2 m) behind the scenery to throw the silhouettes of the actors onto the screen.

When you reach the end of the play, have the narrator tell the story while the actors silently go through the motions of the final scene behind the curtain. Only their shadows and the light of Popocatepetl's candle will be visible to the audience. If you want to give your actors lines to speak, rather than have the narrator read all of the dialogue, try to capture some of the flowery language of the legend in your script. Don't make the speeches too long or difficult, though, or they will be hard to memorize. Here are a few sample lines of dialogue from the scene at the ball, when Popocatepetl declares his love for the Princess.

Popocatepetl: Oh great King! I am here at your feet, I, Popocatepetl, to make a great request. You know me—I have frequently and bravely fought for you. You know that my arm is strong and that, as long as I have breath in my body, I will fight for you.

King: It is true. You have won many fierce battles for our kingdom. What do you ask of me?

Popocatepetl: I must ask you for a treasure more priceless than all of your riches. Oh King, a single desire haunts my days: to marry your daughter, the beautiful Princess Izia. My heart beats only for her!

Princess: Father, you must know . . .

King: Silence! Popocatepetl, I know of your great courage and loyalty. But, of course, my daughter is of noble birth and cannot marry a warrior. However, I feel respect and friendship for you, and since you are truly the bravest soldier in the kingdom, I will give you a chance to prove yourself and win my daughter's hand in marriage.

The Legend of Popocatepetl can be performed on stage in 6 scenes. In each scene the narrator fills in the background information as the action progresses.

Scene 1: The Ball. The King, the Princess and their attendants enter the palace. The King sits at his throne, the Princess at his side. You can play lively Mexican music during their entrance.

Next the soldiers enter, led by Popocatepetl. You can play some marching music for the soldiers' entrance.

When all of the cast is on stage you can have dancers perform for the court (see the description of the Mexican *raspa* on page 55).

The captain and the Princess watch each other throughout the scene. When the dancing ends the captain approaches the throne and, on his knees, asks to marry the Princess. The King explains his plan and leaves the stage followed by the members of the court.

Scene 2: Popocatepetl and the Princess are alone together. He declares his love. She gives him her scarf. Popocatepetl takes it, kisses it and marches off to war as she waves farewell.

Scene 3: The narrator describes the passage of time as the Princess goes from the window to her bed at the left of the stage and back again. Her attendants enter and attempt to comfort her and bring her food, which she refuses to eat.

Scene 4: The King enters. The Princess asks for news and he tells her that the captain has died. She falls back on the bed and shuts her eyes. The attendants weep.

Scene 5: Military music plays and shouting is heard offstage. The entire cast enters and talks excitedly about the victory. Popocate-petl enters to cheers from the crowd and approaches the King, who tells him the bad news. Popocatepetl breaks the arrows he carried on his back in a quiver and throws them on the floor. He demands to see the Princess and is led to her funeral bed. The King and the other members of the court leave the stage quietly. Popocatepetl grieves aloud as he kneels by the dead Princess.

Scene 6: Performed as shadow-theatre as described above. The spotlight placed behind the screen is turned on, showing the shadow of the captain who holds the Princess in his arms. He places her on the table which represents the summit of the mountain. The captain takes a lighted candle (handed to him from offstage) and holds it with his arm upraised. Soft, sad music plays in the background as the narrator explains the meaning of the legend.

THINGS TO MAKE

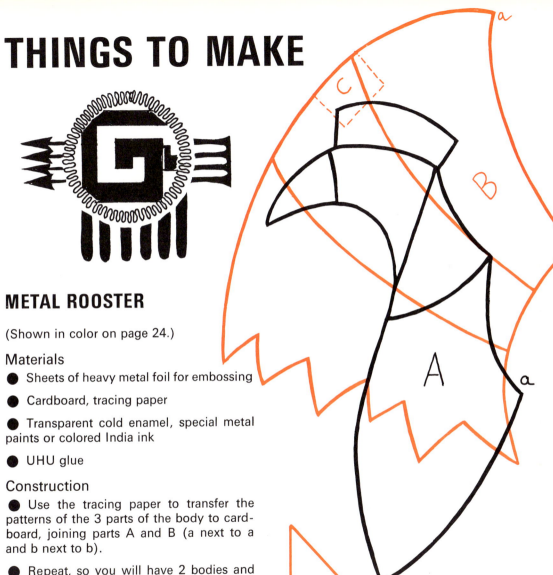

METAL ROOSTER

(Shown in color on page 24.)

Materials
● Sheets of heavy metal foil for embossing

● Cardboard, tracing paper

● Transparent cold enamel, special metal paints or colored India ink

● UHU glue

Construction
● Use the tracing paper to transfer the patterns of the 3 parts of the body to cardboard, joining parts A and B (a next to a and b next to b).

● Repeat, so you will have 2 bodies and 2 feet.

● Cut out the silhouettes and the feet.

● Glue the 2 body sections together, one on top of the other, and slip the feet in place between the halves where shown by

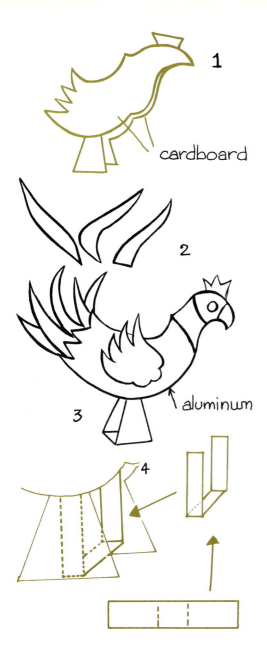

1

cardboard

2

3

aluminum

4

the dotted section C in the pattern (see Drawing 1).

● Cut small pieces from the metal foil sheets to cover the different parts of the rooster body. Since the pieces must overlap, like tiles on a roof, cut more than the section to be covered; about $\frac{1}{4}$ inch (6–7 mm) larger all around the edge of the body is enough.

● The wings and the tail are made from strips of metal foil cut in the shape of feathers of various lengths. Use shapes which make the feathers appear to be moving (see the examples in Drawing 2).

● You can decorate the different pieces of metal by embossing with a dried-out ballpoint pen (using the technique described on page 15).

● Spread glue on the inner side of each metal piece. Glue them in place.

● Slip the tail feathers between the cardboard section and the pieces of metal which cover it; the wings fit in between 2 of the metal sections.

● Let the glue dry completely, then decorate with transparent cold enamel, which gives a beautiful luminous effect (you can also use India ink).

If the bird is to be hung as a mobile, you must decorate both sides.

If you wish to simply stand it up, give it greater stability by separating the legs and glueing a strip of cardboard folded in a "U" shape between them.

INDIAN IDOL

(Shown in color on page 24.)

This statuette accompanies Indian dances on festival days. Afterwards, the dolls are given to the children.

In Mexico the statuettes are sculpted from pieces of soft wood, then painted in vivid colors. You can make them from cardboard.

Materials

● Thin cardboard

● Square piece of thin wood, 3½ inches (9 cm) on each side

● Some feathers from a feather duster, if you have one. If you don't, use small colorful strips of paper curled between your thumb and a scissor blade.

● Gouache paints

● Tracing paper

Construction

● Use the tracing paper to copy the design of half the statuette body shown at right.

● Draw a vertical line on the cardboard. Retrace the half pattern on each side of this line to make the full outline.

● Color with gouache paints. Let dry.

● Cut out the figure.

● Place it on another piece of cardboard and trace the outline with a pencil. Cut this out also.

● Glue some feathers to the back of the painted outline, sticking out beyond the hair line.

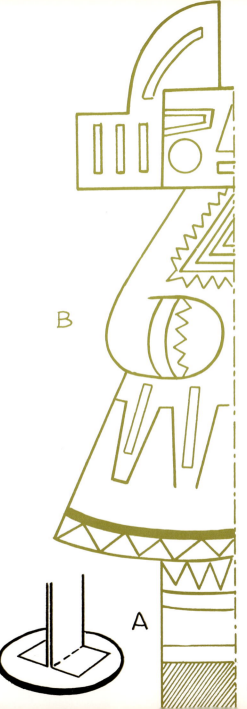

67

● Glue the 2 cardboard outlines together, except for the shaded section of the pattern. Then fold out this part and glue it on top of the wooden square, which serves as a stand (paint this with gouache before glueing).

EMBOSSED METALLIC CANDLESTICK

(Shown in color on page 24.)

This project produces a lovely decoration for the dining room or hall table.

CANDLESTICK

Materials

● Cardboard tube $4\frac{1}{4}$ inches (10.5 cm) high and $1\frac{3}{4}$ inches (4.5 cm) in diameter (use the roll from aluminum foil or bathroom tissue)

● 2 circles of cork, cardboard or wood, 4 inches (10 cm) in diameter

● Metal foil for embossing

● Dried-out ballpoint pen

● Compass for drawing circles

● Glue

● Tracing paper

● Clip-type clothespins

● Newspapers

Construction

● Cut tabs $\frac{3}{8}$ inch (10 mm) deep all around the tube (Drawing 1).

● Open the tabs out (Drawing 2), coat them with glue and attach them to the cork

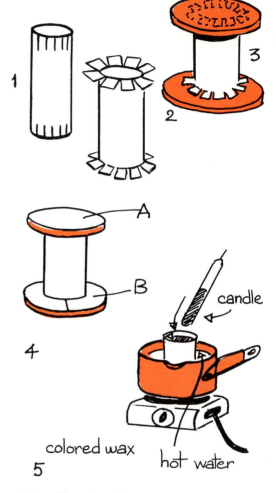

circles (Drawing 3). Hold the construction together with clothespins while it dries.

● Cut a band $3\frac{1}{2}$ x $6\frac{1}{2}$ inches (8.5 x 16 cm) from the metal sheet.

● Copy the design for embossing shown on page 69 with tracing paper.

● Put the metal sheet down on a thick

newspaper and place the sheet of tracing paper over it.

● Retrace the design with a dried-out ballpoint pen.

● Remove the tracing paper and carefully inscribe the metal to give the forms a rounded appearance. Keep working until the design is clear and attractive.

● Spread glue on the cardboard tube and roll the band of embossed metal around it.

● With the compass draw 2 circles with 4 inch (10 cm) diameters on a sheet of metal foil. On one of them draw a second, inner circle with a 2 inch (5 cm) diameter. Decorate the circles with a design of embossed triangles and lines.

● Cut out the circles.

● Glue the solid circle to the top side of the candlestick (A in Drawing 4).

● Cut out the central circle of the second piece by cutting a slit from the outside edge and cutting out the middle. Place the ring you obtain around the tube and glue it on the upper surface of the candlestick base as shown at B in Drawing 4.

● Heat the bottom of a candle, let a little wax drip on the middle of the top of the candlestick and stand the candle up quickly in the melted wax, holding it until the wax hardens.

CANDLES

You can use either plain white candles or colored candles.

You can also make candles yourself in the

Design for embossing

colors of the Mexican flag (green, white, and red) by following these instructions.

Materials

- Saucepan with water

- Stove or hot plate

- Plain white candles

- Food colors, red and green, or special candle colors, if available

- 2 tall, thin jars (olive jars, for example)

Procedure

- Melt a white candle in a jar placed in a saucepan of simmering water.

- When the wax is melted, add the red coloring.

- Dip another white candle to be colored in the liquid wax, taking it out quickly so that the lower third of the candle is tinted red (Drawing 5).

- Melt another white candle in another jar, and set in simmering water. Tint it with a little green color.

- Take the candle with the red base and dip the top end in the melted wax, removing it quickly. When the wax hardens you will have a candle with a green top, white middle and red bottom.

- Attach it to the top of the candlestick as described above.

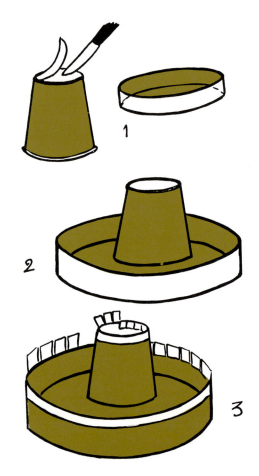

MEXICAN HAT

(Shown on page 24 and on cover.)

This typical Mexican hat can be used as a dresser tray or pencil holder.

Materials

- Cover from a circular cheese box. If this is not available, make a similar piece by cutting out a cardboard circle with a 6-inch (15 cm) diameter and a cardboard band 1½ inches (4 cm) wide and 19 inches (48 cm) long. Cut tabs ½ inch (1 cm) deep along one edge of the band, about ½ inch (1 cm) apart. Bend the tabs at right angles, staple the ends together to form a circle and glue the tabs to the bottom of the cardboard circle, making an upright lip 1 inch (3 cm) high

● Green construction paper

● Paper cup or yogurt container, preferably in solid yellow

● Narrow green plastic adhesive tape

● Orange adhesive-backed paper

● Transparent glue; sharp knife

● Gouache paints in hot pink and white

Construction

● Turn the paper cup over and use a sharp knife or X-Acto blade to neatly cut off the bottom (Drawing 1).

● Glue it, top edge down, in the middle of the cheese box cover (Drawing 2). Let dry.

● Paint the inside of the cup and the cover hot pink.

● Cut a band, the height of the lip of the cover and long enough to fit around, from green paper. Glue it in place.

● Stick half of the green adhesive tape's width around the outside edge of the cover. Cut notches in the upper half and press them down inside the edge (Drawing 3).

● Decorate the top edge of the cup in the same way.

● Cut out some triangles from the orange adhesive paper and glue them in place on the outside edge of the hat and at the top of the crown, as shown in the photo on page 24.

BEADED NECKLACE AND LOOM FOR WEAVING BEADS

(Shown in the photos on page 73 and 75.)

The Huichol Indians are especially skilled in making jewelry, necklaces, bracelets, and belts of small beads either threaded or woven.

You can use the sample design here for your choice of a necklace, bracelet, headband, or even a belt. You merely reproduce the design over and over again until you reach the required length.

First, here are the plans for constructing a small loom for weaving with beads. This loom is inspired by an Indian design.

THE LOOM

Materials

● 2 pieces of wood $5\frac{1}{2}$ x 2 inches (14 x 5 cm) and $\frac{1}{2}$ inch (12 mm) thick

● 2 round wooden rods $18\frac{1}{4}$ inches (46 cm) long and $\frac{3}{8}$ inch (1 cm) in diameter (spindles or turnings available at lumber yards or hobby shops)

● 4 screw eyes

● Sandpaper

Construction

● Drill (or ask an adult to drill) 2 holes, slightly smaller than the spindles you bought, at a point $\frac{3}{8}$ inch (1 cm) from the side and bottom of the wood block (see Drawing 1, next page). Drill both blocks.

● On the bottom of the wood rectangles, make notches with a knife, spaced $\frac{1}{16}$ inch (1 mm) apart.

● To make the rods fit easily into the drilled holes, sand them slightly with sandpaper to make the ends slightly narrower and tapered.

● Attach the screw eyes in place $\frac{3}{8}$ inch (1 cm) in from the edges, in the middle of the board's thickness (Drawing 2). Do this on both boards.

WEAVING WITH BEADS

Materials

● Very fine linen thread

● Special needle for threading beads

● Small beads in all colors

● Necklace clasp (sold in many hobby shops), or an ordinary button

Assembling the Warp

● Tie the thread to one of the screw eyes and coil the thread around the loom, placing it into each of the notches (Drawing 3).

● You must thread as many lines as the number of bead rows you plan on, plus 1. For example, for the pattern on page 73, the 11 rows of beads required 12 threads. The threads must be strung in notches directly across from each other so that they are parallel to each other.

● Finish by tying the thread to another screw eye.

THE WEAVING

● Thread a needle with linen thread. Tie the end of the thread to a thread of the warp and start weaving in and out 4 or 5 lines without beads (Drawing 4).

● Thread the beads which make up the first row of the design, in order.

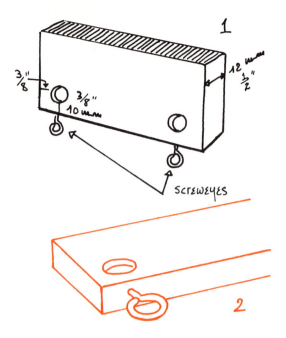

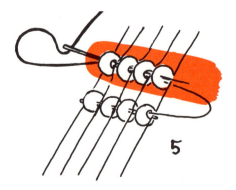

● Place your finger under the warp and fit each bead between 2 threads of the warp.

● Run the needle back through all of the beads, which you keep raised on your index finger. The needle must pass above the warp threads, thus holding the beads in place (Drawing 5).

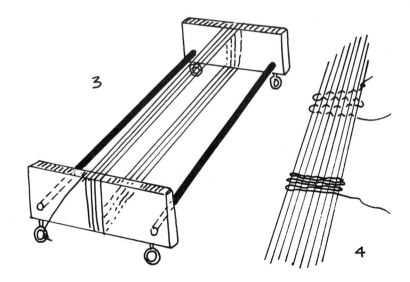

3

4

● Continue in this way, carefully following the order of beads in the design.

● When you get to the end of the weaving thread, tie the end solidly to one of the warp threads and tie a new weaving thread to the same warp thread. Hide the knots between the beads.

● To finish off the string of beads, make another few rows of weaving thread without beads before stopping to hold the beads in place.

● Cut the strings of the warp 2–2½ inches (5–6 cm) from the end of the weaving. Thread them back through the unbeaded end rows, weaving in and out one thread at a time. Cut off any excess.

PUTTING THE NECKLACE TOGETHER

● Sew one side of the necklace clasp on each end of the beaded strip, or sew a button on one end and make a loop of thread at the other end.

The length of the loom described here is sufficient for weaving bracelets, necklaces, chokers and headbands.

If you want to weave a belt, you will have to weave 2 or 3 sections (depending on the waist size needed) and assemble the pieces with small tight overcast seams of linen thread joining the edges. Plan the length of each of these sections keeping in mind the repetition of the design, but remember that you can also plan some solid rows or simple stripes in different colors to break up the pattern.

AZTEC WARRIOR

(Shown in color on next page.)

This decorative panel is inspired by a Mexican design.

Materials

● Wooden board or thick cardboard, about 10 x 8 inches (25 x 20 cm)

● Strips of wood $\frac{3}{32}$ inch (4 mm) thick (balsa wood sticks are fine)

● Wooden circle about 4 inches (10 cm) in diameter and $\frac{5}{16}$ inch (8 mm) thick

● 36 nails with large heads, $\frac{3}{16}$ inch (1.5 cm) long

● Some straws or straw reeds if you can find them (if possible use only "natural" materials for this project)

● Chamois cloth, suede or leather remnants

● Feathers (from a feather duster)

● Linen thread and very fine red cotton crocheting thread

● A little purple adhesive-backed felt

● Transparent glue

● Black matt gouache paint

Construction

SHIELD

The main element of this panel is the shield which is made on the wooden circle using the technique of stretching strings between nails.

● Cover the wooden circle with a circle of adhesive-backed felt.

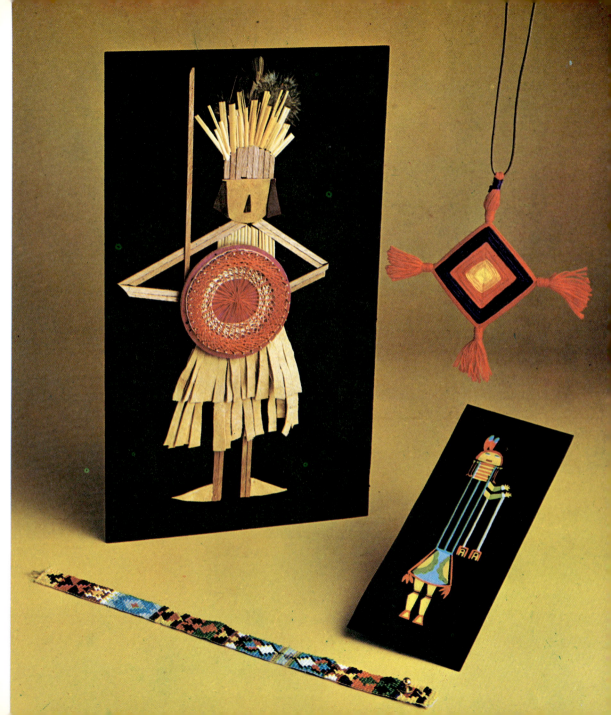

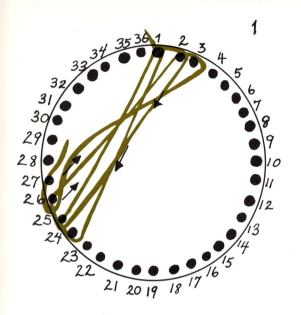

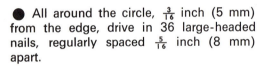

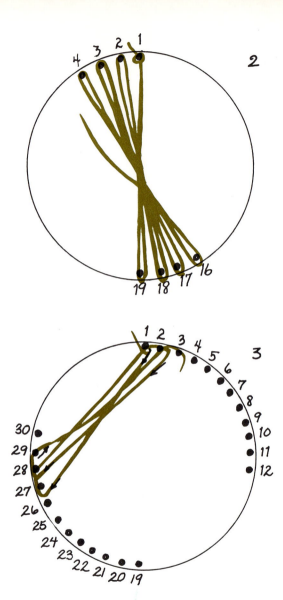

● All around the circle, $\frac{3}{16}$ inch (5 mm) from the edge, drive in 36 large-headed nails, regularly spaced $\frac{5}{16}$ inch (8 mm) apart.

● The thread decoration is made up of 3 layers, one over another.

First layer: Tie the linen thread to nail no. 1 (Drawing 1). Run the thread to nail no. 24, around behind 24 and 25. Return to nail no. 1 and pass behind 1 and 2. Then across to no. 25 and behind 25 and 26. Return and pass behind 2 and 3, then cross back around 26 and 27. Continue this pattern all around until all the nails have been threaded around.

Second layer: Do with the red crochet thread. This layer is made up of simple figure-8's crossing in the middle. Begin at nail no. 1, cross to the left side of no. 19, pass behind this nail and across to the right

side of no. 2, around and then across to no. 18, around and back to no. 3 and so on (Drawing 2).

Third layer: Again with the red crochet thread, follow the same system of threading you followed for the first layer but change the interval, beginning with a thread from no. 1 to no. 27 and continuing around the circle (Drawing 3).

THE WARRIOR

● Paint the 10 x 8 inch (25 x 20 cm) background panel black. Let it dry completely.

● Cut the shape of the face from a leather remnant (Drawing 4). Glue it in the middle $\frac{7}{16}$ inch (11 mm) from the top of the panel.

● From very small scraps of leather cut out the nose and hair and glue them in place (Drawing 4).

● The base of the helmet is made of wooden strips cut following the general shape of the outline and glued in place.

● Above these strips glue some short feathers at their bases.

● Overlapping on the feathers glue irregular pieces of straw, $1\frac{1}{4}$–2 inches (3–5 cm) long. Cut and flatten these straws with a knife and glue only at the base, leaving the top loose to give some depth to the helmet.

● Following the photograph, glue on the arms, made up of wooden strips laid at an angle.

● Make the torso with straws, cut open and flattened and glued side by side.

● For the skirt, take 2 rectangles of chamois cloth or suede about $3\frac{1}{4}$ x $2\frac{1}{2}$ inches (8 x 6 cm). Cut the bottom edges into large fringes. Glue the rectangles down, one over the other with the fringes overlapping

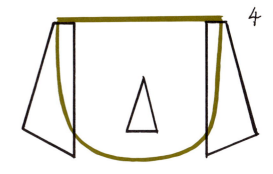

(see color photo on page 75). Glue only the top edges, leaving the fringes free.

● Glue on a long wooden strip to represent a lance.

● Put the strips for the legs in place and glue them.

● The feet are 2 triangles of leather or chamois. Glue them to the background about $1\frac{1}{4}$ inches (3 cm) above the bottom edge of the panel.

● Finally spread glue on the back of the shield and put it in place. Hold it down firmly until the glue sets.

SMALL MASK

(Shown in the photo on page 79.)

In Mexico you will find many small objects made of clay, such as this little face which you can make very easily.

Materials

● Large, smooth, oval pebble to serve as a mold

● Self-hardening modelling clay

● Spatula or modelling tools

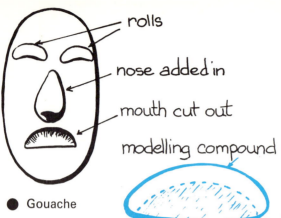

rolls

nose added in

mouth cut out

modelling compound

pebble

- Gouache
- Aluminum foil

Construction

● Place the pebble on a sheet of aluminum foil.

● Take a small ball of modelling clay, about the size of a large nut. Knead it between your fingers until it is smooth.

● Cover the top and sides of the pebble, being careful to spread the clay to an even thickness. Do not cover the bottom.

● Add small rolls for the brow and the nose. Work the joints smooth with your modelling tools.

● Carve out the mouth with a tool.

● Allow to dry leather-hard. Remove the pebble carefully without deforming the mask.

● Allow to dry completely, for 1 or 2 days.

● Paint with bright gouache colors.

You can, of course, make several masks, varying the expressions on the faces. Try to find examples in Mexican art books for inspiration.

LITTLE MEXICAN MAN LAMP

(Shown in the photo on the next page.)

Materials

● Lamp socket with wire and plug attached

● Round white light bulb, large but of low wattage such as those used in large make-up mirrors

● Lampshade for a bedside lamp with 2 wire rings which clamp around the light bulb (Drawing 2).

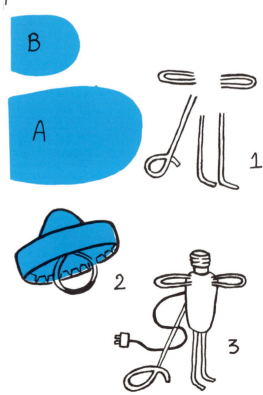

B

A

1

2

3

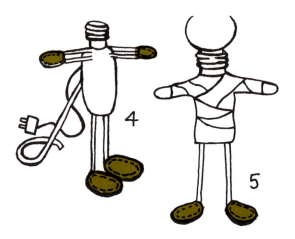

- Self-hardening modelling clay

- Iron wire (metal coat-hanger wire is fine)

- Felt: black, light green, blue, beige

- Red rick-rack trim

- Band of gauze

- White fabric glue

- Wire cutters and pliers

Construction

● With pliers and wire cutters prepare the 5 wire sections shown in Drawing 1, using the dimensions given.

● Shape the modelling clay into a cylinder about $3\frac{1}{2}$ inches (8.5 cm) high and $1\frac{1}{2}$ inches (3.5 cm) thick.

● Stick the wire pieces in place in the modelling clay. Push the lamp socket into the top of the clay, making sure it is held securely (Drawing 2).

● Cut 4 copies of pattern A (feet) from blue felt and 4 copies of pattern B (hands) from beige felt.

● Sew them together 2 by 2 and glue them around the wire stems (Drawing 4).

● Wrap gauze around the arms and torso of the figure to give it some bulk (Drawing 5).

PANTS

● Cut pattern C twice out of black felt.

● Join the 2 pieces with an overcasting seam (Drawing 6).

● Place the pants on the figure and sew the outside seams closed (Drawing 7).

● Glue a strip of rick-rack trim on the side of each pants leg (Drawing 8).

VEST

● Fold a piece of black felt. Prepare pattern D, placing the dotted line on the fold in the fabric. Cut two identical patterns in this way.

● On each folded piece sew the sides and sleeves from a to b using an overcast stitch (Drawing 9).

● Join the 2 pieces together with a seam down the back from c to d (Drawing 9a).

● Trim with rick-rack as in the photo.

● Hide the base of the lamp socket with a small band of felt glued or stitched in place.

SARAPE (CAPE)

● Cut a rectangle $4\frac{3}{4}$ x $9\frac{1}{2}$ inches (12 x 24 cm) of thin green felt (or another brightly colored fabric).

● Glue on horizontal felt bands to decorate the *sarape.*

● Fold the band as shown in Drawing 10 and attach it to the shoulder.

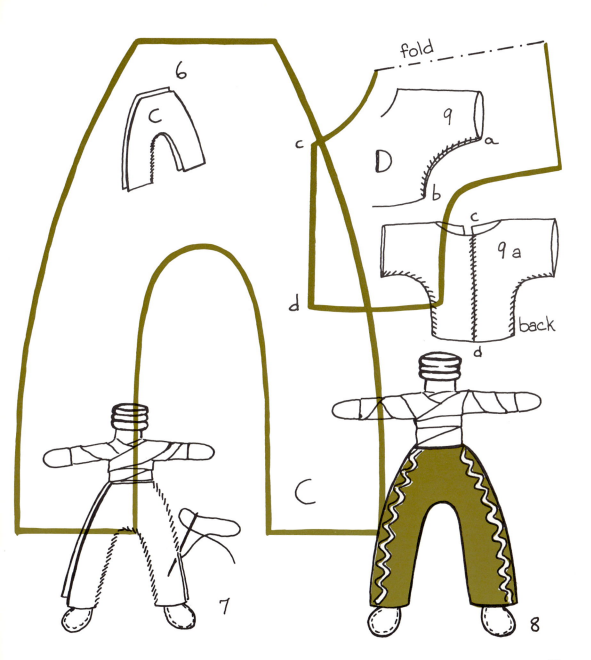

6

C

fold

9

D

a

b

c

9 a

d

back

d

C

7

8

HEAD

● Cut a small moustache from black felt and glue it onto the light bulb (Drawing 11).

● Make the hat by glueing a light-colored felt band around the edge of the lampshade (Drawing 12). Notch the lower edge of the band so it can be glued on easily. Glue each notch inside the shade.

TREE OF LIFE

(Shown in color on the next page.)

This is a symbol of the Pueblo Indians, representing the principle of life until death. The Indian artisans make them in all sizes, with varying numbers of branches.

Materials

● Self-hardening modelling clay, such as Marblex or Mexican Pottery Clay (which dry in the air)

● Wooden rod 10–12 inches (25–30 cm) long (you can use a very straight tree branch)

● Iron wire (coat hangers are fine)

● Large pebble

● Matt white water-base paint, gouache, varnish

Construction

● Cut pieces of iron wire and wrap them around the wooden rod, spacing them as shown in the drawing. Attach each piece securely.

● Stand the assembly up on a large pebble embedded in a thick layer of modelling clay. Make a base large enough to keep the tree standing securely.

● Work the plastic modelling clay into several sausage-shaped rolls. Use these to cover the iron wires.

● Cover the central trunk with small pieces of clay.

- Distribute this layer evenly over the entire surface of the tree (using a wooden spatula or other modelling tool). Avoid over-thickness or hollow spots. Be especially careful to smooth around the branch joints.

- With your fingers form abstract shapes of birds with the clay.

- Place them on the branches, moistening the mounting spots before attaching them. Look at the illustrations for an idea of placement.

- Let the construction dry for 2 or 3 days.

- If some cracks develop during the drying, fill them in with fresh modelling clay. However, the water-base paint you will use will fill up most of the unevenness and cracks.

Decoration

- Paint a coat of matt white paint over the entire tree and the birds. Let dry.

- Decorate with gouache paints in lively colors as shown in the drawing. The design should be very elaborate.

- You can, if you wish, use clear varnish made for covering gouache to complete the decoration.

MASK NOTE PAD

(Shown in the photo on the next page.)

Try out your embossing skill on this decorative reminder plaque which makes a unique gift or an item to sell at a Mexican festival vendor's booth.

The mask can be made in the size of the

iron wire

modelling compound

wooden rod or branch

pebble

Sheet of heavy metal foil for embossing, either copper or aluminum

Pencil; glue

Small pad or supply of note paper

Leather strap for hanging

Embroidery or other sharp scissors; stapler

Construction

Use tracing paper to transfer the half pattern of the mask shown on page 85 to a sheet of metal foil, simply turning the paper over to transfer the right side of the mask. Emboss the design as described on page 15.

Use embroidery scissors to cut out the open areas (mouth and eyes).

Fold a small metal band in three lengthwise and shape it around a pencil. Glue it in the middle of the bottom edge of the cardboard backing.

At the back top of the backing attach the leather strap with staples.

Glue the burlap (hessian) flat on the front of the board.

Glue the mask and note pad in place as shown in the photo.

pattern shown here, or it can be enlarged using the square transfer method (page 95) to make a large decorative panel.

Materials

Cardboard rectangle 8 x 5½ inches (20 x 14 cm)

Piece of burlap (hessian) the same size

DECORATED MIRROR

(Shown in color on page 79.)

When they are very young, Mexican children learn to make beautiful pictures with colored yarn.

Here, inspired by this technique, is a decorative frame for a pocket mirror.

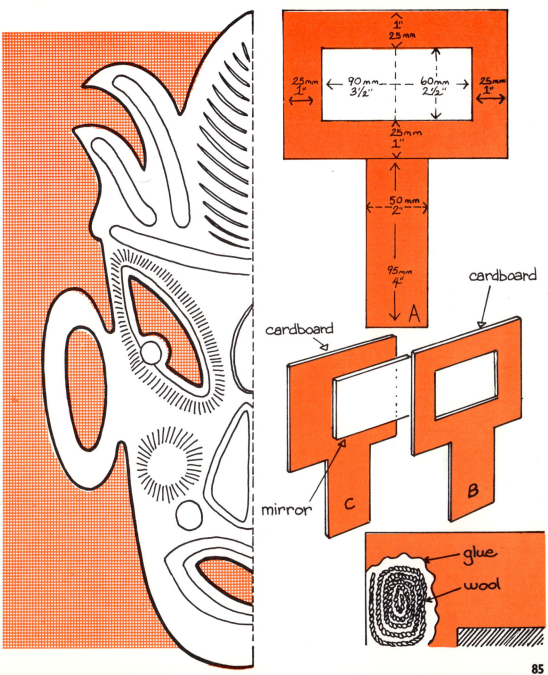

1"
25 mm

25 mm
1"
←— 90 mm —
3½"

60 mm
2½"

25 mm
1"

25 mm
1"

←— 50 mm —→
2"

95 mm
4"

A

cardboard

cardboard

mirror

C

B

glue

wool

Materials

● Pocket mirror, $3\frac{1}{2}$ x $2\frac{1}{2}$ inches (9 x 6 cm)

● Tapestry yarn in small skeins: light green, purplish blue, olive green, orange, jade green

● White fabric glue, transparent glue

● Cardboard (from a shoebox, for example)

● Clip-type clothespins

Construction

(Drawings on page 85.)

● Cut pattern A out of cardboard twice, following the dimensions shown.

● In one piece cut a window as shown in Drawing B, $3\frac{1}{2}$ x $2\frac{1}{2}$ inches (9 x 6 cm). Do not make an opening in the other piece C.

● Glue the mirror in the middle of piece C.

● Spread glue over the rest of the surface of piece C and place piece B on top. Press firmly (or hold them together with clothespins) until the glue sets.

Decoration

● Cut strands of wool of different colors and lengths.

● Spread the fabric glue on the top surface, covering small areas at a time.

● Roll up the woollen strands and place them on the glued areas (arrange them with the point of a scissors). Make different interesting shapes. Cut off the surplus wool.

Do not let the cardboard show through— push the strands together tightly.

PAINTED BIRDS

(Shown in the photo on page 79.)

Display these birds in the middle of a large wooden pot with cacti growing in sand and gravel.

Materials

● Pebbles, plastic foam balls, or other small, round or oval objects

● Self-hardening modelling clay

● Gouache or cold enamel

● Matt white water-base paint

Construction

If the pebbles themselves have amusing shapes which remind you of a bird or an animal, simply paint and decorate them accordingly.

If not, proceed as follows.

OWL

● Cover an oval pebble completely with modelling clay, forming at the same time a

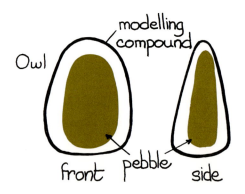

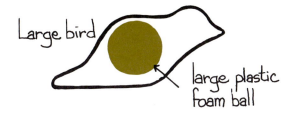

Large bird

large plastic foam ball

SMALL BIRD

● Model completely with modelling clay, without an inner support.

● Decorate after it dries completely.

WOOLLEN HANGING

(Shown in color on page 75.)

This hanging reproduces a design often used in Mexico, since the woollen cross represents an important religious symbol. Its name is *El Ojo de Dios,* or the eye of God. It is the witness to the actions of human beings.

You can wear it as a pendant or hang it as a decoration.

Materials

● Fine wool or cotton for knitting, shiny or dull: orange, violet, deep yellow and light yellow (or other bright colors can also be used)

● Large (burnt) match used for fireplaces, 12 inches (28 cm) long, or 2 small square

base which is large and flat enough so that the owl can stand up straight (see drawing).

● Allow to dry for 2 or 3 days. The dried clay takes on the look and feel of stone.

● Paint directly with gouache or apply a base coat of white water-base paint first.

● Allow the base coat to dry, then paint on a design with gouache or cold enamel (for inspiration see page 79). Always use bright colors.

LARGE BIRD

● Make this bird using a plastic foam ball with a 1½ inch (4 cm) diameter as a base.

● Cover the ball with modelling clay. Add a small ball of clay and form the head, neck and beak.

Shape your bird following the silhouette in the drawing. Be sure the details (neck, beak and tail) are not too thin or they will break off during drying.

Smooth the clay to be sure it doesn't have any small cracks.

● Let dry completely before painting.

● If possible, paint a base coat of water-base paint before painting with gouache. Choose nice bright colors.

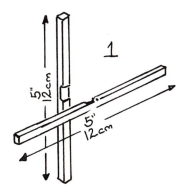

1

5" 12 cm

5" 12 cm

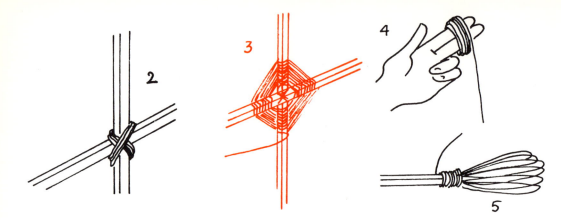

balsa wood strips $\frac{1}{16}$–$\frac{1}{8}$ inch (2–3 mm) thick, as used by model builders

● Sharp knife

Construction

● Cut 2 wooden strips from the match 5 inches (12 cm) long. At the middle of each make a notch with the knife. Be sure not to cut too deeply into the wood (Drawing 1).

● Place a little glue in the notches. Place the sticks at right angles, fitting the notches together, and hold until the glue sets.

● With yellow cotton or wool wrap the crossbar very tightly, binding the 2 sticks together (Drawing 2).

● Wind the wool once around each bar, without tightening, proceeding around the cross and working outwards.

● After several turns, change the color. Tie the 2 colors together with a double knot hidden behind the crossbars. Continue the winding without tightening (Drawing 3).

● Change the color as many times as you like. Each time the knot should be hidden as well as possible.

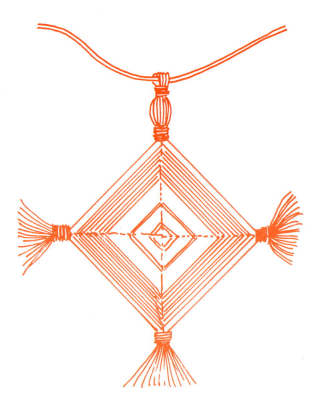

● When you get to the end, tie the last thread neatly to a bar (if necessary put a drop of glue on the knot to keep it from slipping).

● To make a pom-pon, roll the yarn around 2 fingers for a dozen turns (Drawing 4). Remove the roll from your fingers and place it on the end of the crossbar. Wrap yarn of the same color around the roll and crosspiece very tightly to hold it in place (Drawing 5). Tie and cut off the excess yarn.

● Cut through the loops of the roll to make a tassel.

● Repeat this procedure at 3 points of the cross.

● At the fourth point don't cut through the loop. Instead, pass a leather lace or woollen cord through so you can hang your creation.

This design can easily be made in larger sizes using longer and stronger sticks, or very small with sticks $2-2\frac{1}{2}$ inches (5–6 cm) long.

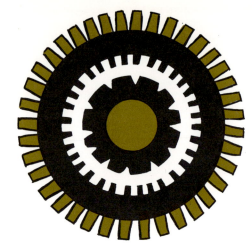

APPENDIX

RECIPES

HOT CHOCOLATE
Serves 4 to 6

Cooking time: 10 minutes

5 tbsp. (75 ml.) of cocoa powder. 1 qt. (1 l.) skim milk. 1 tbsp. (5 ml.) powdered cinnamon. 6 sugar lumps.

Dissolve the powdered cocoa in the milk.

Add the cinnamon and sugar.

Bring to a boil, stirring constantly.

Cook for 5 full minutes until it thickens.

TORTILLAS

Preparation time: 10 minutes

Cooking time: 1 hour

For 40 tortillas: *2 cups (230 g.) cornflour. 2 cups (230 g.) wheat flour (regular flour). 2 eggs. Half a water glass of club soda (carbonated water). ½ cup (125 g.) melted butter. Glass of water. Salt.*

Pour the 2 flours into a large bowl. Make a well in the middle and break the eggs into it. Mix thoroughly with a spatula.

Add the glass of water, a pinch of salt, half glass of club soda and the melted butter.

Mix until you have a thin, smooth batter. Let stand 30 minutes.

Heat a frying pan or griddle, coating the surface with a little butter. Fill a ladle with batter and pour it into the hot pan, spreading it out as much as possible. Brown on both sides.

Repeat until batter is used up.

GUACAMOLE

Preparation and cooking time: 30 minutes

1 tomato. 1 avocado. 1 pimento, mashed. Chervil, minced. Salt. 1 large onion, chopped.

Dip the tomato in boiling water, then peel and mash it.

Mash the avocado and mix with the tomato.

Add the chopped onion, minced chervil, salt and mashed pimento.

Mix well. Chill and serve.

Guacamole is an extremely popular Mexican sauce served in many different ways:

● In a *taco,* a rolled *tortilla* filled with sauce, then fried

● With white rice

● In a dish with *tortillas,* covered with sauce, then wrapped around with slices of ham, and served with white rice

● As a garnish with meat.

XOCHIMILCO SALAD
Serves 6

Preparation time: 30 minutes

Cooking time: 20 minutes

2 lb. (1 kg.) boiled potatoes. 2 avocados. 2 hard-boiled eggs. 1 tomato. 2 bunches of radishes (about 8). 2 tsp. (10 ml.) capers. Sour cream. Oil and vinegar. Salt and pepper to taste. Worcestershire sauce.

In an earthenware bowl, prepare a dressing with 2 tbsp. (30 ml.) of oil, ¾ tsp. (3.75 ml.) vinegar, salt and pepper, 1 tbsp. (15 ml.) sour cream, ¾ tsp. (3.75 ml.) Worcestershire sauce, and some capers.

Clean the radishes and slice them.

Wash the tomatoes and cut them in slices.

Peel the avocados and dice them finely.

Cut the hard-boiled eggs and the boiled potatoes.

Mix all ingredients together. Serve chilled.

AN OUTDOOR DINNER

Get a portable barbecue or make one yourself with a large steel drum.

Punch holes in the side of the drum and place a wire grill or grating on top.

Fill with an ample supply of charcoal. Light, and wait till there is a bed of glowing red coals before starting to cook.

PEPPERS AND EGGS
Preparation time: 10 minutes

Cooking time: 15 minutes

1 pepper per person. Sour cream. 1 egg per person. Salt and pepper.

Cut the peppers in half, remove the membrane and seeds.

Place a tablespoonful (15 ml.) of sour cream in each hollow and break an egg on top of each. Season with salt and pepper.

Balance the prepared peppers carefully on the grill. The coals should not be too hot— the peppers should cook gently.

The eggs will set slowly. When they turn white, they are ready to eat.

SKEWERED MEAT
Serves 4

Preparation time: 20 minutes

Cooking time: 10–15 minutes

$1\frac{1}{2}$ lb. (680 g.) lamb or mutton, boneless leg or shoulder (you can substitute beef, chuck or sirloin if you prefer), cubed. 2 lb. (1 kg.) green peppers. 1 lb. (453 g.) onions. Several small red pimentos. 2 avocados.

On metal skewers place: a chunk of meat, a piece of pepper, a tomato chunk, a slice of onion, a piece of avocado, a pimento. Start over in the same order until the skewer is filled. Push the ingredients together tightly.

Brush with the Mexican sauce described below.

Broil the skewers over the glowing coals.

Season generously with salt and pepper.

Serve with a cream sauce or additional Mexican sauce if you desire.

GRILLED BANANAS
Preparation time: 5 minutes

Cooking time: 10 minutes

1 banana per person. Powdered sugar. A little lemon juice.

Place the unpeeled bananas on the grill.

When they become very black, cut the skin down the length with a sharp knife.

Remove a strip of the peel and sprinkle with sugar. Moisten with a few drops of lemon juice.

MEXICAN SAUCE
Preparation time: 10 minutes

Cooking time: 15 minutes

2 cups (500 ml.) cooking oil. 1 tbsp. (15 ml.) strong mustard. 2 lb. (1 kg.) onions. 1 pepper. 1 bunch celery. 4 cloves garlic.

Mince finely the onions, garlic, celery and pepper.

Place all the ingredients in a saucepan. Heat over a low flame and cook gently until the mixture forms a sort of paste. Season with salt and pepper.

This sauce is delicious when brushed on meats on the barbecue or chicken on the rotisserie.

MEXICAN NATIONAL TOURIST OFFICES

United States

Norman Williams Contrearas
3443 N. Central Avenue
Financial Center
Suite 101
Phoenix, Ariz. 85012

Sergio Guerrero Ochoa
219 Sutter Street
San Francisco, Calif. 94108

Herman W. Elger
Gold Mall 46
Cinderella City
Englewood, Col. 80110

William Cobb
1156 15th Street N.W.
Suite 423
Washington, D.C. 20005

Wilbert C. Sanchez Herrera
100 Biscayne Boulevard
Suite 612
Miami, Fla. 33132

Antonio Rivas Mercado
Peachtree Center
Cain Tower—Suite 1201
Atlanta, Ga. 30303

Jose Luis Sanchez Navarro
John Hancock Center
Suite 3615
Chicago, Ill. 60611

Elva Licea Tapia
One Shell Square Building
Concourse Level
New Orleans, La. 70130

Vincent Hodgins
405 Park Avenue
Suite 1002
New York, N.Y. 10022

Terry Butler Weber
3501 Harvard Avenue
Dallas, Tex. 75205

Canada

Guillermo Ponce, Regional Director
1 Place Ville Marie, Suite 2409
Montreal H3B 3M9, Quebec

Jorge Sanchez Vidauri, Regional Director
85 Richmond Street WL.
Toronto 110, Ontario

Carlos Hampe, Regional Director
700 West Georgia St.
Vancouver V7Y 186, British Columbia

England

Mona King, Delegate
52 Grosvenor Gardens
London SW1W 0AX

Australia

Ricardo Zalapa, Representative
105 George St.
Sydney, N.S.W.

SQUARE TRANSFER METHOD

If the design you have chosen is not the size you want it to be, you may enlarge or reduce it by this grid method. To enlarge a design, for example, draw a $\frac{1}{4}$ inch- (.6 cm-) grid, which is simply a series of criss-crossed lines $\frac{1}{4}$ inch (.6 cm) apart, over the design to be enlarged. On another piece of paper, draw a 1 inch- (2.5 cm-) grid—criss-crossed lines 1 inch (2.5 cm) apart—using the same number of squares as the $\frac{1}{4}$ inch- (.6 cm-) grid. Sketching freehand, copy the lines within each of the small squares of the $\frac{1}{4}$ inch- (.6 cm-) grid to each of the squares of the 1 inch- (2.5 cm-) grid. The $\frac{1}{4}$ inch- (.6 cm-) and 1 inch- (2.5 cm-) grids increase the original design four times.

By varying the size of the grids, you can vary the final size of your design. Reverse the size of the grids—that is, draw a 1 inch- (2.5 cm-) grid over the original design and transfer the lines to a $\frac{1}{4}$ inch- (.6 cm-) grid—to reduce the design to one quarter the original size.

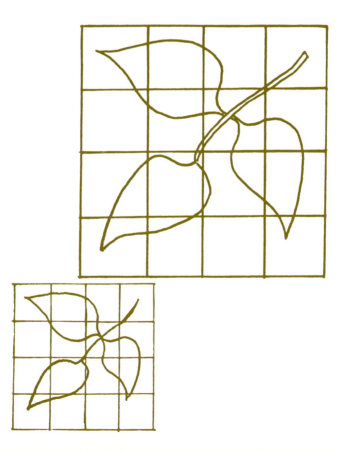

INDEX